Nationalism in Europe since 1945

Studies in European History Series

Studies in European History
Series Standing Order ISBN 978–0–333–79365–7
(outside North America only)

You can receive future titles in this series as they are published by placing a standing order. Please contact your bookseller or, in case of difficulty, write to us at the address below with your name and address, the title of the series and the ISBN quoted above.

Customer Services Department, Macmillan Distribution Ltd,
Houndmills, Basingstoke, Hampshire, RG21 6XS, UK

Nationalism in Europe since 1945

André Gerrits

First published 2016 by
PALGRAVE

Palgrave in the UK is an imprint of Macmillan Publishers Limited, registered in England, company number 785998, of 4 Crinan Street, London, N1 9XW.

Palgrave Macmillan in the US is a division of St Martin's Press LLC, 175 Fifth Avenue, New York, NY 10010.

Palgrave is a global imprint of the above companies and is represented throughout the world.

Palgrave® and Macmillan® are registered trademarks in the United States, the United Kingdom, Europe and other countries.

ISBN 978–1–137–33787–0

This book is printed on paper suitable for recycling and made from fully managed and sustained forest sources. Logging, pulping and manufacturing processes are expected to conform to the environmental regulations of the country of origin.

A catalogue record for this book is available from the British Library.

A catalog record for this book is available from the Library of Congress.

Printed in China

Contents

Introduction

The large majority of studies on nationalism either discuss nationalism *in abstracto* or identify it with its most extreme expressions only, in the form of 'hot' nationalist conflicts and wars. This book on nationalism in Europe after the Second World War is both narrower and wider in scope. It talks about nationalism as a *political* phenomenon. Political nationalism is defined as political action plausibly guided by a distinct idea of the nation or a strong sense of national identity. This is largely irrespective of the form and content of political action. It can either be tolerant or intolerant, left wing or right wing, defensive or offensive, governmental or oppositional. Simultaneously, however, this study takes a wider scope than is usual in publications on nationalism, by linking nationalism with major processes of change in post-war Europe. Nationalism is discussed in relation to processes of European integration, to the development of the welfare state, to the theory and practice of communist rule in Central and Eastern Europe and to the rise of globalization and immigration after the Cold War. This approach has the advantage of situating and contextualizing nationalism in real-world changes. Nationalism never comes alone. But it has disadvantages too. Nationalist ambitions typically merge with other concerns, which gives nationalism its multifaceted nature and much of its popular and political allure, but which also makes it difficult to isolate from other beliefs, motives and justifications of political behaviour. Euroscepticism, anti-communism and support for or critique of the national welfare state or multiculturalism can be inspired by a range of political beliefs, besides nationalist ideas. Still, situating the national issue in the larger context of post-war European history reveals more about the actual role and relevance of political 'nationalism' than limiting the discussion to only an abstract or theoretical level.

1

The writing of the history of the nation has been intertwined with the construction of the nation. In the nineteenth century, history as a modern discipline began as 'national' history. Nations and nation states were the evident points of reference for most historians. They were the inspiration, the subject and the target of historical research. Notwithstanding the many different approaches that have been developed over time, the state and the nation have remained as the dominant emphases of historical science. Most history is still national history. This presents the historian of nationalism with methodological challenges. Nationalism is a pre-eminently international phenomenon. It is unique to every country, but shared by many countries. The historian of nationalism in Europe has to go beyond the 'national', without losing sight of what is crucially important to every discussion on nationalism and national identity: the individual nation.

The nature of the series in which this book appears is to discuss actual historical developments, and to provide a historiographical overview. The political approach to nationalism that this study takes steers both of these aims in specific directions. It discusses those aspects of the nationalism debate that have a direct bearing on its role and relevance in European politics since 1945, and it engages mostly with those studies that are particularly important to the nationalism-as-politics orientation. To control for the lack of a temporal balance in nationalism research and to prevent a post–Cold War interpretative bias, earlier publications will be an important source of information both on the history of nationalist thought and behaviour in Europe after the Second World War, and on how earlier generations of historians understood its relevance.[1]

---

[1] This study elaborates on my earlier research on nationalism, especially [52].

2

1 The Debate on Nationalism

The days of nationalism have largely passed, concluded the British historian John Breuilly in the early 1980s [16: 352].[1] To the extent that nationalism still had political significance in Europe, he wrote, it was mainly in the form of separatism, and then only in a limited number of countries. Integration and transatlantic cooperation in the Western part of the continent and communist rule in Eastern Europe had largely, perhaps definitively, removed the traditional power and relevance of nationalism. Breuilly's idea was widely shared among other scholars on contemporary European history. Nationalism was considered an anachronistic and anomalous political ideology. It had long lost its nineteenth-century progressive and emancipative connotation, and it was now pre-eminently associated with the atrocities of two world wars and with the experiences of fascism and National Socialism. After the Second World War, a widespread desire for renewal had manifested itself across war-torn Europe. The eradication of the destructive force of radical nationalism was a common aspect of the otherwise strongly diverging post-war political regimes in East and West. The liberal international order under American dominance provided the Western part of Europe with three decades of uninterrupted and unprecedented economic growth and rising prosperity. And Soviet communism and internationalism seemed to lift the poorer countries of Eastern Europe out of their state of underdevelopment and poverty. The new reality worked. The days of nationalism were finally over – or so it seemed.

---

[1] In the second edition of his book (1993), Breuilly recalls this statement and qualifies it in the light of the range of nationalist movements that had meanwhile been involved in the collapse of the Soviet Union and in events elsewhere in Eastern Europe. Both editions of *Nationalism and the State* are referred to throughout this book.

Throughout most of the post-war decades, nationalism continued to be seen as politically and intellectually offensive. The elimination of nationalism was a major source of inspiration and legitimacy for the European integration effort. In terms of European identity building, post-war Europe's major negative 'other' was especially its own past, its history of conflict and war. Four decades later, once the Cold War had ended, the upsurge of nationalism in post-communist East-Central Europe was widely perceived as another major argument for the widening of European integration. Membership of the European Union would further extend Europe's social and economic progress into the east of the continent. But while the virulence of post-communist nationalism in Eastern Europe could still be dismissed as convulsions of old conflicts and other dark times, the resurgence of radical nationalism in many member states of the European Union around the same time came as a shock and as an embarrassment. Apparently, European integration had not fully eliminated radical political nationalism within its member states. In fact, European integration had created its own and novel variant of political nationalism: Euroscepticism and anti-Europeanism.

The processes of cooperation and integration in Western Europe and the establishment of communist regimes in Eastern Europe had fundamentally changed the old continent, with clear ramifications for political nationalism. During the first post-war years, the spirit of the time was internationalist. Nationalism was generally associated with the horrors of the past, or with the world outside Europe. The negative assessment of nationalism was part of the dominant notion of societal and political modernization, including the belief that traditional boundaries within and between states and societies would gradually fade. Traditional lines of division between religious or ethnic groups would give way to functional divisions of a socio-economic or political nature. Dividing lines between states and nations would lose relevance because of increasing cross-border contacts and cooperation. It seemed that both West and East in Europe, through very different trajectories, had reached a post-national phase of historical development.

Reality proved considerably more complicated. The nation and the national state would survive as the key political frameworks in post-war Europe. And after the Cold War, nationalism would revive again, initially in the (former) communist countries, which experienced an unprecedented moment of national resurgence and state formation, but later also in Western Europe. From the 1990s, different manifestations of nationalism would shape politics again in the whole of the continent, more so perhaps than they had done at any time since the Second World War.

The post-war history of Europe is divided along geographical, political, and chronological lines. From 1945, the division between the communist and capitalist (and partially democratic) parts of the continent was generally perceived as a partition between East and West in Europe. Geographical borders had become political ones, and vice versa. This East-West division lasted until the early 1990s. The end of the Cold War, the disintegration of the Soviet Union, and the later enlargement of the European Union ended the division of Europe between two essentially different, opposing, and hostile political regimes. However, the continent remained far from whole. Old boundaries were removed or faded away, but others remained, and still others re-emerged. The geopolitical East-West division of Europe vanished with the collapse of communism, but would be replaced by a larger number, and a greater diversity, of democratic governments among the member states of the European Union, and a wider range of non-democratic regime types beyond the union. Economically too, Europe changed rapidly, mostly due to the transformation of the communist command economies, the enlargement of the European Union's internal market, and the massive expansion of Russia's energy sector and exports. All in all, Europe became less divided but more diverse. This study on nationalism is largely organized along Europe's post-1945 lines of division. It distinguishes between Cold War and post–Cold War Europe, studying Western and Eastern Europe separately for the former period and mostly together for the latter one.

The two-dimensional partition of European history since 1945, between the Cold War and the post–Cold War era and between communist and capitalist Europe, deeply affected nationalist thought and action. Post-war nationalism was faced with challenges that had been wholly or partly unknown during earlier periods of Europe's history. The establishment of communist regimes in Eastern Europe was the most important example. Communist rule changed nationalism in Eastern Europe but never eradicated it. Nationalism remained prominently present throughout the communist era in various guises, often underground, but occasionally also conspicuously and explicitly present, as an instrument of communist leaderships to repress opposition and to acquire popular support. But also in Western Europe, political nationalism endured, buttressed by reactions to a multitude of largely new phenomena such as American predominance, European integration, non-European immigration, and growing ethnic and cultural diversity. All these developments had a lasting impact on the nations of Europe, on the national states, and on nationalism. Post-war political nationalism developed against the backdrop of these historic changes. It was impacted by, and itself impacted upon, these larger developments from 1945 onwards.

Nationalism proved resilient and flexible. It would take different forms in different eras and in different parts of post-war Europe. Measuring it on a scale of radicalism, 'banal' or everyday nationalism can be found at one end and 'hot' or violent nationalism at the other end of the scale. Soft or 'banal' nationalism [13] has occasionally been defined as patriotism. Scholars have extensively debated the differences between nationalism and patriotism. The distinction often boils down to a normative one: nationalism is supposedly 'bad', while patriotism is 'good'. Patriotism is seen as a variant of nationalism without the unconditional loyalty and the strong sense of exclusiveness that defines 'real' nationalism. Patriotism is often identified with the civic understanding of the nation, as 'loyalty to a political unit' [7: 178], rather than to an ethnic community. In this book, as in most studies of nationalism, greeting the flag, singing the national hymn, and other everyday indicators of national allegiance receive less attention than radical manifestations of nationalism. However, expressions of intolerant and violent nationalism such as ethnic cleansing, xenophobia, or racism are not the only demonstrations of nationalism examined here. In Western and Eastern Europe, during most of post-war history, nationalism took passive or restrained forms, and it manifested itself in the context of different views, from anti-communism to Euroscepticism, from populism to xenophobia.

Nationalism is shaped by its wider ideational context. Nationalist arguments by East European communists were different from those expressed by West European liberals or conservatives. As the context evolved, so too did the specific content and the direction of nationalist opinions. The political purpose and relevance of nationalism remained rather similar though, throughout most of the post-war history of the continent, which is to mobilize political support and to strengthen and legitimize political power.

In communist Eastern Europe, nationalism was officially considered a typically capitalist, bourgeois political sentiment, a remnant of the past which communism would soon eliminate. In Eastern Europe, lack of academic freedom made serious research into the contemporary relevance of nationalism impossible. In Western Europe, academic interest in nationalism was largely determined by the perceived political relevance of nationalist thought, and this was generally considered to be low during the first post-war decades. With relatively few albeit important exceptions [4; 16; 49], it took until the end of the 1980s before nationalism became a staple of academic study. And from the 1990s, research on nationalism exploded. Historians and political scientists alike, inspired by the collapse of communism, which offered fresh opportunities for historical research, and the perceived role of nationalism in the disintegration of the Soviet Union and Yugoslavia, took a renewed interest in the topic. Academic interest followed real-world change.

In the aftermath of the Second World War, few researchers [26] foresaw a continuation of nationalism in Europe. German scholars, in particular, living in their defeated and divided homeland, heralded the end of nationalism and the national state. In a lecture in Münster in July 1953, the prominent historian Theodor Schieder signalled that 'the era of the national state in Europe was over' – 'this is an undeniable historical truth' [146: 285]. Others were equally insistent, and not without a touch of regret: 'How much the role of nations has meanwhile changed', Eugen Lemberg [107: 10] wrote, just five years after the end of the Second World War. 'Sovereignty and self-determination hardly exist anymore .... Reasonable men join together and give up part of the sovereignty rights, which they still passionately defended only a few years ago'.

As the years passed, only a handful of scholars regretted the dearth of academic research on nationalism. During the early 1970s, the British sociologist Anthony Smith observed how 'surprisingly little attention' the subject had received by social scientists [154: 3]. Wrongly, he opined. 'Of all the visions and faiths that compete for men's loyalties in the modern world, the most widespread and persistent is the national ideal' [155: 1]. In his perception, the so-called 'demise of nationalism' in the mid-twentieth century had been more apparent than real [155: 152–3]. Despite the fact that by the early 1980s nationalism still was a peripheral and scattered field of academic research, some of the most noticeable studies were published during this decade. Writing in 1990, shortly before the Soviet Union and Yugoslavia collapsed and the political map of Eastern Europe would change beyond recognition, one of Britain's most prominent historians, Eric Hobsbawm, still argued that Europe was actually witnessing the further decline of nationalism, if not the end of the era of the national state. 'Historians are at least beginning to make some progress in the study and analysis of nations and nationalism', he wrote, '[which] suggests that, as so often, the phenomenon is past its peak. The owl of Minerva which brings wisdom, said Hegel, flies out at dusk. It is a good sign that it is now circling round nations and nationalism' [69: 183]. As a Marxist historian, Hobsbawm may have been inspired by ideological considerations and by the wish to see the traditional nation state disappear, but his conclusion on the essentially anachronistic nature of nationalism was not yet very controversial. The zeitgeist in early post–Cold War Europe was internationalist, if not universalist. But while the national state seemed to have lost practical significance, the continent also experienced a historically unprecedented process of state formation. More than 25 new countries were formed after the Cold War, considerably more than in the wake of the Great War and the collapse of Europe's empires, another historical moment of state formation. In direct contrast to Hobsbawm's predictions, nation, national identity, and nationalism in Europe had actually acquired a political virulence that they had not had for a very long time, neither in the Eastern nor in the Western part of the continent.

From the early 1990s, the actual relevance and topicality of nationalism in Europe could no longer be denied. Nationalism studies became the hot topic of research agendas across the continent. Researchers referred to a 'fourth wave' of nationalism research, inspired by the break-up of the Soviet Union and Yugoslavia [59: 144–5]. Similar to earlier waves of research, nationalism studies retained a strong normative element. Researchers reverberated in their fundamental critique of major aspects of contemporary nationalism – its claims, its ambitions, and its consequences. Notions such as national identity, which had been long ignored either as largely outdated or as only one among the multiple identities that individuals have (and most probably not the most important one), resurfaced, but with scepticism.

Practically every scholar emphasized nationalism's multifarious nature, but few scholars [13; 167; 185] considered its neutral, positive, or pro-democratic properties. Nationalism was not necessarily good or bad, they argued against the stream. Nationalism derives its quality from the intentions of its proponents, and from the consequences of their actions. Nationalists, not nationalism, kill people [185: 214].

A political definition

In 1945, the American historian of German-Jewish descent Hans Kohn (1891–1971) published *The Idea of Nationalism*. It would become one of the most influential studies of nationalist thought and practice. Kohn suggested a typological distinction between a predominantly cultural or ethnic concept of the nation and a political interpretation of the nation, which he defined as civic nationalism. He situated ethnic nationalism mostly in Eastern Europe, while civic nationalism originated in Western Europe, in England and France in particular, from the late eighteenth century. Kohn defined the civic idea of the nation as the collective sovereignty of the people of a given state, of all people, irrespective of race or ethnicity. Initially, nationalism remained essentially liberal and secular, at least until the 'Spring of Nations' in the mid-nineteenth century. As nationalism spread eastwards though, Kohn asserted that it lost its original political and integrative character. In contrast to Western Europe, where the borders of nations and states were fairly closely aligned, large multinational empires with ethnically diverse populations dominated the Eastern part of the continent. The prevailing concept of the nation in Eastern Europe could therefore not be politically defined, by citizenship, but only culturally or ethnically, by descent. In the multinational empires of nineteenth century, Central and Eastern Europe (and *mutatis mutandis* in most of their successor states after the First World War) nations were generally differentiated by ethnicity, that is, by language, religion, history, and other cultural criteria. In the context of nationalism, ethnicity should primarily be understood as a variant of perceived solidarity through time, or, as the German language so aptly puts it, as *Schicksalsgemeinschaft*, a community of fate.

Following Kohn, the civic idea of the nation could be viewed as rational and historically progressive, because it unites people within the framework of the national state, while ethnic nationalism may be considered as divisive and parochial, since it undermines and fragments the national and international order. The civic-ethnic contradiction in the nationalism debate maintained its paradigmatic significance throughout the post-war history of Europe. It offered an attractive combination of analytical clarity with value judgement. It served descriptive and normative goals. The armed confrontations in the Caucasus and elsewhere in the Soviet Union and the full-scale wars in former Yugoslavia from the mid-1980s were often seen through the prism of this dichotomy. They were considered as the result of anachronistic, pre-modern, and ethnic national antagonism – as typically 'non-Western' conflicts.

But irrespective of the lasting 'popularity' of Kohn's ideal-typical distinction, it has also been consistently criticized as overly dichotomous as too rigid, and too normative or moralistic. Many historians agree that the civic and ethnic definitions of the nation are changeable. They tend to overlap, and are often difficult to separate. No type of nationalism is exclusively civic or ethnic. In reality, nationalism is profoundly ambiguous. No single case of civic nationalism is devoid of ethnic or cultural features, and practically every manifestation of ethnic nationalism has civic, that is political, legal, and institutional, features. Moreover, both civic and ethnic nationalisms can be inclusive and exclusive, albeit often on different criteria. Liberal democratic nations such as France and the United States, relatively open societies with a predominantly civic approach to citizenship, did not start out that way. Civic nationalism can be as inflexible and rigid as its ethnic alternative. It can demand that minorities surrender major aspects of their culture and heritage in order to be accepted as full and equal members of the national community. Firm and sometimes impenetrable barriers can stand between ethnic background and legal status. For most of Germany's post-war history, the dominant 'ethnic' definition of the nation made it practically impossible for Turkish or other non-ethnically German immigrants to receive citizenship. On the other hand, people of German descent from far-flung places such as Kazakhstan or Central Asia automatically received German citizenship upon their arrival in the country.

The differences between civic and ethnic ideas of the nation are a matter of 'more or less' rather than 'either-or' [185: 32]. The idea of the exclusively civic nation not only 'gets the history wrong', as Bernard Yack asserts, but it also fails to acknowledge that every nation relies on civic, legal, and rational arguments in combination with an affirmation of a cultural or ethnic identity [185: 23]. Yack also critiques the notion of civic nationalism on normative grounds. It is a 'flawed political idea', he argues, flawed for its basic neglect of the idea of a 'community of shared principle'. He negatively compares civic nationalism with patriotism. 'Republican patriotism', as Yack phrases it, is more than a moderate, benign, or acceptable form of nationalism. It is distinctive from ethnic nationalism because it takes the political ideals of citizenship very seriously, and it differs from purely civic nationalism in its 'collective passion' for the fatherland, the 'republican patria' [185: 40].

Europe after the Cold War showed how fluid and ambiguous this distinction between the different variants of nationalism is in practice. Examples abound of ethnically inspired nationalism in the Eastern, former communist part of the continent, from the anti-Armenian pogroms in Baku and other places in Azerbaijan in the early 1990s in the wider context of the Nagorno-Karabakh conflict, to the crimes against different population groups in Bosnia and Kosovo during the Yugoslav civil wars in the middle and late 1990s. But the extensive process of state formation that followed the mostly peaceful disintegration of the Soviet Union also bore witness to the strength of civic nationalism and ethnic tolerance in Eastern Europe. Similarly, in Western Europe, the ethnic or cultural variant of nationalism re-emerged suddenly and unexpectedly. From the 1980s, the notion of a national identity that should primarily be understood in cultural terms (with references to ethnicity and religion) became an ever more prominent aspect of regular, mainstream politics in Western European countries, advocated and encouraged by increasingly vocal and prominent nationalist parties.

Before introducing the political definition of nationalism that will be used in this book, it is important to raise the question how nationalism links with other, related notions such as the nation and national identity. Kohn [97] proposes a clear causality, asserting that a certain idea of the nation (ethnic or civic) suggests a specific nationalist behaviour, namely integrative or divisive. Anthony Smith concurs with this interpretation, asserting that nationalism is the doctrine 'that makes the nation the object of every political endeavour and national identity the measure of every human value' [156: 18]. The basic idea is that nationalism *prioritizes* and *politicizes* the nation and national identity. But what is the nation, and what is national identity? 'Nations', Smith suggests, 'are felt and lived communities whose members share a homeland and a culture' [159: 12]. Smith's concept of the nation is built on a combination of objective and subjective factors. It refers to what individuals collectively 'feel', based on what they apparently 'share'. So the nation is as much about a common language or religion, about common (political) institutions and territory, as it is about their perception and interpretation. This combination of the real and the perceived or imagined also informs Smith's understanding of a third crucial concept, that is national identity [156: 9]. Nationalism and national identity are different, though related, phenomena. A strong national identity, based on a particularly persuasive narrative of the nation, past and present, does not necessarily translate into a strong sense of nationalism. Sweden and other Scandinavian countries are often considered as strong on national identity but generally moderate on nationalism [93: 153]. In spite of this, as Smith [156: vii] points out, '[w]e cannot begin to understand the power and appeal of nationalism as a political force without grounding our analysis in a wider perspective whose focus is national identity'. There are assumptions and ambitions that are common to all ideas of the nation, to all nationalists. These include, but are not limited to, a shared territory or homeland, common memories and myths, a shared mass culture, common legal rights and duties for all citizens, and a shared economy. From these commonalities, Anthony Smith derives his combined definition of the nation and of national identity as

> the continuous reproduction and reinterpretation by the members of a national community of the pattern of symbols, values, myths, memories and traditions that compose the distinctive heritage of nations, and the variable identification of individual members of that community with that heritage and its cultural elements [156: 18].

National identity remains one of the most fundamental, inclusive, and widespread collective identities in the modern world. However, the nation is rarely the only or an exclusive kind of collective cultural or political identification. National identity typically overlaps with other characteristics such as religion, class or social group, ethnicity or language, and political and professional affiliations. Such identification may influence the nature of one's national identity but, as Anthony Smith concludes, it 'rarely succeeds in undermining its hold' [156: 143].

Nation, nationalism, and national identity belong to the category of 'big structures, large processes, and huge comparisons' [169]. Precisely because these are such variable, changeable, and contested concepts, with obvious scholarly and moral connotations, nearly every author on nationalism presents his or her own definition, which is mostly a reworking of an earlier classification by another scholar. There are practically as many definitions of nationalism as there are studies on nationalism. This work starts from the widely applied *political* definition of nationalism. This political explanation focuses on the role and significance of nationalist thought and ideas throughout the political process, from motivations and incentive for political action, to specific political ideas and arguments, and, most importantly perhaps, to the legitimization of political behaviour. Nationalism politicizes the nation; it turns the nation into 'a political subject' [106: 9].

However, even among the scholars who accept nationalism as an essentially political phenomenon, there is no agreement on the specific nature and significance of it. Is it an idea, an idiom, a belief, or perhaps an ideology? The British historian Eli Kedourie famously stressed the ideational origins and nature of nationalism. Paraphrasing the East Prussian philosopher Immanuel Kant, Kedourie defined nationalism as a doctrine of self-determination. A good man is an autonomous man, and for a man to be autonomous, he needs to be free. 'Self-determination thus becomes the supreme political good for man' [95: 29]. Smith argues that nationalism is best defined as a 'belief system', either as 'a programme of action to achieve and sustain the national ideal' or as a movement that translates this idea into political action [155: 3]. Ernest Gellner for his part explains nationalism as a 'theory', especially a theory of political legitimacy ([49: 1]; see also Wehler [176]).

Can we also take the argument a step further and define nationalism as an ideology? Most authors would hesitate. Guided by specific intellectual traditions and ideas, nationalism does contain features of an ideology, Michael Freeden [45: 750] argues, but of a pseudo-ideology or an 'ideology-lite'. Nationalism resembles a 'thin-centred' ideology, 'limited in ideational ambitions and scope'. Differing from a full ideology, nationalism lacks the set of coherent principles and ideas that logically and compellingly link political motivations, strategies, and outcomes. Rather than being an ideology in its own right, nationalism links up with other ideologies. 'When nationalist ideas are found in host ideologies, they reflect the features of the host', Freeden [45: 759] asserts. It is therefore more appropriate to refer to nationalist discourse within a given ideology, than to talk about liberal, conservative, or communist nationalism *per se*. This relates to the 'parasitical' nature of nationalism. In post-war European history, nationalism is mostly shaped by, and receives its ultimate power through, the broader political orientation that it allies with, that it supports or opposes. Also for this reason, John Breuilly maintains that nationalism is at most a doctrine, not an ideology. Nationalism is a doctrine which seeks, exercises, and legitimizes state power, based on the assumption that the specific values and interests of the nation take precedence over most other political beliefs and concerns. Breuilly's definition, which is echoed in this book, is broad enough to include the real-world issues that will be discussed in the following pages, but it is not so general that it loses any specific meaning. As Breuilly helps us to remember: 'We need clear definitions and distinctions, but equally we must not forget that these express our analytical needs rather than neatly reflecting the "real" world' [17: 402, f. 9].

To explain nationalism as a form of politics almost automatically implies its positioning as a typically modern phenomenon. This connects with another major division in the nationalism debate, between the 'modernist' and the 'primordialist' interpretations of nationalism. Modernists claim that nationalism is typically a response to the deep societal and political changes from especially the early nineteenth century. Primordialists emphasize the historical, long-term nature of nationalism. They maintain that nationalism, or actually the ethnic identities that underpin the idea of the nation, is really part of human nature, irrespective of any time frame [157: 40–1]. Among the scholars who stress the essentially modern nature of nationalism, materialist and ideational interpretations compete. While the former are essentially structural, the latter leave more room for agency, for the consequences of human

14

behaviour. Ernest Gellner is probably the most prominent representative of the modernist approach. Gellner perceives nationalism as a response to the uneven processes of modernization in nineteenth-century Europe. Capitalist development, urbanization, and industrialization inspired and allowed for the creation of 'standard national cultures', thereby dramatically increasing the relevance of identity, and of national identity in particular [49: 121]. Karl Deutsch is another advocate of the modernization thesis. Nationalism comes with modernization because of its popular appeal and political attractiveness, he argues. Nationalism fulfils an emotional need in the individual and a legitimating service for the political elite [37: 33]. The sociologist Liah Greenfeld defines nationalism as the 'constituent element of modernity'. 'It is the symbolic blueprint of modern reality, the way we see, and thereby construct, the world around us, the specifically modern consciousness' [63: 159, 161]. Greenfeld stresses the reciprocity of structure, ideas, and agency in nationalism – an approach that is shared in these pages. Social structures, she argues, including political collectives, owe their existence to individuals' belief in them, and their character to the nature of their ideas. In nationalism, this is manifested in social structures and cultural traditions.

Defining nationalism as a form of politics also lends it a strongly functionalist connotation. Functional approaches to nationalism emphasize the role it plays in the context of modern statehood, often linked with the above-mentioned challenges of modernization. Nationalism would provide a sense of identity, of belonging and togetherness in times of rapid and dramatic change, thereby specifically serving the interests of political elites. It is the integrative aspect of nationalism which turned it into such a particularly powerful instrument in the hands of all kinds of different political leaders, including, as will be argued, the communist regimes of Eastern Europe. In this respect, as Breuilly suggests, the function of nationalism may not be very different from the purpose of ideas or ideologies within political movements in general: coordination, mobilization, and legitimation [17: 93]. Coordination combines different interests in one political movement through the formulation of common ideas and goals. Mobilization brings these groups into politics, and legitimation is supposed to provide them with an 'acceptable image' to outsiders. As we will see, these three aspects continue to apply to nationalist movements in post–Cold War

Europe, including the populist and radically nationalist parties in the countries of the European Union.

Among the functionalists in the nationalism debate, political legitimation is considered as nationalism's main purpose [85: 13, 23]. Few historians present the functionalist or instrumentalist argument more forcefully than Hobsbawm. 'Nationalism comes before nations', he argues. 'Nations do not make states and nationalisms but the other way around' [69: 10]. Hobsbawm's interpretation of nationalism seemed wholly in line with the fateful experience of interwar Europe, when authoritarian and totalitarian regimes used the state apparatus to pursue sometimes viciously repressive policies of national and political identity building. It also appeared to concur with the political events that shook Europe around the time Hobsbawm published *Nations and Nationalism since 1780,* in 1990. In various republics of the Soviet Union and in Yugoslavia, nationalism evidently went ahead of the 'nation' or national identity. Arguably, there was no widely shared concept of a Belarusian nation, probably not even of a shared Belarusian identity, when the independent state of Belarus was established in August 1991. The Belarusian 'state', that is the intellectuals, politicians, artists, and others who were involved in the process of state formation, had to invent the Belarusian nation and to popularize its identity. The Central Asian republics of Kazakhstan, Uzbekistan, Turkmenistan, and Tajikistan, which gained independence around the same time, were actually constructs of the Bolshevik regime during the 1920s. Moldovans never really enjoyed a strong sense of 'nation-ness', and they probably began to identify themselves as 'Moldovans' only after the establishment of the Moldovan Soviet Socialist Republic, part of the Soviet Union, in August 1940, if not later, after the independence of the Republic of Moldova in August 1991. The situation in some of the former Yugoslav republics was not very different. In Bosnia, despite the fact that the Muslims distinguished themselves religiously from their Catholic and Orthodox neighbours, the Croats and Serbs, the national state preceded the nation and national identity. The situation in the independent republic of Macedonia (officially named as the Former Yugoslav Republic of Macedonia, as a gesture towards Greek national sentiment) was not essentially different either. Attempts at nation building followed state formation.

While Hobsbawm's rigid functionalist argument struck a positive chord with all those who observed nationalism's unexpected significance in Western and Eastern Europe with alarm, it met with serious critique among other nationalism scholars. Gellner [49: 186] agreed that nationalism indeed invented nations, but then only on the basis of 'pre-existing differentiating marks'. Smith [159: 88] critiqued Hobsbawm's explanation of nationalism as a form of invented tradition because it left 'no room for emotion or moral will, not even on the part of the masses', who in Hobsbawm's interpretation seem not much more than passive recipients of the state-building designs of the elites. Hobsbawm's interpretation of nationalism was strongly morally inspired. Nationalism had lost its progressive significance. From an engine, a 'major vector' of historical development during the nineteenth century, nationalism had degenerated into a 'reaction ... of weakness and fear', an 'attempt ... to erect barricades to keep at bay the forces of the modern world' [69: 163–4]. But why would nineteenth-century nationalism be understood as progressive and its late-twentieth-century variants as regressive, if not reactionary? Had the Poles more legitimate rights to fight for sovereignty and independence from Tsarist Russia than the Lithuanians had from communist Russia a hundred years later? For the vast majority of Lithuanians, and for many other nations in Central and Eastern Europe, the creation of newly independent or sovereign states in the late twentieth century was not a regression but a major step forward, a moment of tremendous national emancipation rather than a return to history. In their view, nationalism, democracy, and modernity were inseparably connected – as many of their fellow Europeans had believed a century earlier.

Defining nationalism as singularly reactionary or regressive denies its multifarious nature. Also during the post-war history of Europe, both before and after 1989, political nationalism manifested itself as a form of opposition *against* the state and the existing national or international political order, and as an instrument *of* the national state or the ruling elite, to legitimize and consolidate the current situation. Nationalism was crucially important for political actors in power and for those who still aspired to it. There is nationalism which opposes the state and, albeit more difficult to precisely identify among other aspects of state policies, nationalism that supports and sustains the current state and political regime.

Oppositional nationalism has different levels of action. Only in exceptional cases does it challenge the state *per se*. Separatist or irredentist nationalisms that are aimed against the national state remained relatively rare in Cold War Europe. Separatist nationalists are typically members of distinct ethnic or national groups who feel economically or culturally disadvantaged and who seek to secure either increased political autonomy or full independence. From the late 1980s, when separatist ambitions were radically encouraged by the unexpected political changes in most of the communist countries, they regained a sudden and dramatic importance. Separatist nationalism was at the basis of the formation of independent states in large parts of Eastern Europe. After the Cold War, it became the most forceful and consequential variant of nationalism in this part of the continent. It literally changed the political map of Europe. In a certain way, radical anti-Europeanism, to the extent that it supports the dissolution of the European Union, forms another and even more recent variant of this disintegrative nationalism. Fundamental Euroscepticism contains the specifically nationalist belief that every nation requires and deserves full autonomy and self-expression. In the perception of radical Eurosceptics, the European Union not only illegitimately restricts the sovereignty of the state, but it also harms the autonomy, the identity, the uniqueness of the nation. Oppositional nationalist ambitions can be repressive and emancipatory, revolutionary and conservative. The very same nationalism that is progressive and liberating for some people may be a subversive, anachronistic, and regressive belief for others.

Nationalism as a form of politics is closely intertwined with the *problematique* of the state, more particularly with the power and the legitimacy of those who rule the state. The state was and remains the most powerful institution to shape and enforce conceptions of the nation, in all its varieties. In those cases where nationalism is used as an instrument to support or strengthen the state, one may refer to state nationalism. The nationalism of established states or ruling elites was the most significant variant of nationalism in interwar Europe. It gave nationalism its supremely negative reputation. Nazi Germany, Stalin's Russia, despite the veneer of Marxist-Leninist internationalism, Mussolini's Italy, and in their slipstream practically every other authoritarian state in Europe exploited radical forms of exclusivist nationalism during the interwar decades.

Their nationalist arguments were principally aimed against specific 'others' (bourgeois, Jews, foreigners) within and beyond their borders. They served two major, overriding political goals: loyalty and legitimacy. No single variant of nationalism in Europe caused so much conflict and human suffering as state nationalism or '*nationalistischer Etatismus*', as the German historian Karl-Dietrich Bracher [15: 25] branded it. It was especially state nationalism that the initiators of European integration after the Second World War wanted to eradicate, for once and for all.

Its polymorphous nature and the variety of political functions it potentially serves explain why nationalism is 'not a constant but a variable over time' [9: 178]. The relation between nationalism and more general political developments raises multiple questions. Is nationalism caused by or a consequence of political change? Does nationalism shape or is it shaped by larger events? The answer is both. Nationalism is generally triggered by more comprehensive developments, but then motivates action, which creates 'further' events. When party leader Mikhail Gorbachev initiated his reforms in the Soviet Union, from the mid-1980s, he allowed all kinds of new ideas and activities to emerge, including nationalist ones. Eventually, however, nationalism would play an important role in the further weakening of communist rule, and in the disintegration and collapse of the Soviet Union.

Nationalism cannot be seriously discussed in isolation from its perceived counter-images, internationalism and transnationalism [153]. This book starts from the assumption that national thinking and nationalism are formed in permanent interaction with the forces of inter- and transnationalism [57; 164]. Internationalism specifically focuses on ideas and policies at the state level [82: 682; 164: 139]. It is defined as the political commitment to international cooperation and connection, especially between states [72: 1]. Transnationalism refers to peoples, norms, and ideas, but also technologies that cut across national borders, including such diverse issues as migration, the activities of multinational corporations and non-governmental organizations, and political ideas as democracy, sovereignty, and indeed nationalism. Transnationalism and internationalism can be closely linked, but they are not identical, and neither is necessarily opposed to the national state or even to nationalism [58; 72]. One could argue that contemporary nationalism itself is a form of transnationalism, developing alongside globalization [82: 787]. International linkages and integration can serve the national interest, as much as nationalist considerations may encourage internationalist behaviour. Internationalist or universalist claims were causally linked with the specifically nationalist arguments of most pro-independence movements in Europe's colonial empires. The universalist value of national self-determination supported the nationalist claim of independence. The national interests of France and Germany motivated both countries after the Second World War to engage in far-reaching forms of mutual cooperation. They saw no contradiction between their national interests and the interests of 'Europe' – a view which has been held by the larger part of Europe's political elite ever since, albeit with varying persuasion. In the communist countries too, nationalism and internationalism were closely, although ambiguously, related. Ideologically, nationalism was considered anachronistic and reactionary, as alien to socialism. But at the same time all communist regimes used nationalist arguments to bolster and legitimate their rule. The national and the international interests of the communist states, as defined by their ruling elites, were considered fully identical. Officially, there could be no conflict between the individual and the collective interests of states within the *Pax Sovietica*. Reality was very different though, within and between countries. The nature of communism in each individual country was a combination of international similarities and national particularities. Political institutions and official ideology were practically identical in every communist country, but actual policies could vary significantly, including the legitimation of specific national features of communist rule. Political differences were not considered impossible between communist states, but they could only be of a non-contradictory and transitory nature. Relations between communist countries were officially based on proletarian or socialist internationalism and solidarity. In actuality, however, they could be extremely 'un-comradely', conflict ridden, and even violently hostile. During the Cold War, large-scale military aggression in Europe occurred between communist countries only.

Communist-style political internationalism ceased to exist after the Cold War. The alleged 'crisis' of the nation state in Western Europe, a consequence of globalization and European integration, and especially the collapse of communism in Eastern Europe, created space for another form of internationalism though: a dynamic and market-oriented liberal internationalism. There is a gradual and a substantive difference between internationalism, universalism, and cosmopolitanism, three related concepts that are often considered as antithetical to nationalism. Cosmopolitanism is usually understood as a form of global 'citizenship', that is, a way of life, an attitude, which supposedly is neither determined nor limited by national boundaries. In a world of nation states, cosmopolitanism is the most radical form of internationalism, albeit mainly of the privileged individual variant. Universalism is a more politicized concept. It is a political and philosophical idea that motivates political action, especially by the Western powers, particularly also in the early post–Cold War context. Human rights, liberal democracy, and the market economy were all seen as universal notions: that is they were considered as relevant for and applicable to all peoples and cultures throughout the world.

What applies to nationalism goes for internationalism too: it is not tied to any specific political orientation or affiliation. While internationalism as a political creed typically has a progressive connotation, it can be of an outspoken conservative nature too. The Soviet-dominated form of internationalism in East-Central Europe combined ideologically progressive and conservative notions, if Marxism-Leninism and Great Russian expansionism can be identified as such. Additionally, nationalism and internationalism are not necessarily contradictory either. Charles de Gaulle, president of France from 1959 to 1969, has aptly been characterized as a 'conservative internationalist' [72: 24]. France's national interests, as de Gaulle perceived them, were best served by internationalist policies. The neoconservative agenda of the administration of US president George W. Bush (2001–9) also contained a particularistic mixture of conservative and progressive ideas, of nationalist and internationalist thought [160].

A political definition of nationalism probably comes closest to how most Europeans understand their national identity: that is in a political sense, as being members of a political community, defined by the national state. So whether it is about decolonization, the European integration process, regionalism or separatism, the Soviet domination of Eastern Europe, or the collapse of communism, and whether it was peaceful or violent, democratic or authoritarian, elitist or popular, governmental or oppositional, integrative or disintegrative, and state forming or state subverting – it is especially in the variety of its political expressions and consequences that nationalism has been of such particular relevance to the post-war history of Europe.

Definitions are about making choices. A political explanation of nationalism does not imply that the nation and national identity are always and exclusively understood as 'political'. Other dimensions are involved too: culture, religion, history, or ethnicity. Especially after the Cold War, both the political and the cultural concept of the nation (or nationalism) acquired more significance, and they became increasingly intertwined, also in Western Europe. The civic idea of the nation received an increasingly prominent ethnic connotation, and ethnic nationalism acquired more civic or political significance. As will be discussed, the civil wars in parts of the former Soviet Union and in the Balkans from the early 1990s cannot be understood as purely 'ethnic' conflicts. Although they were certainly based in a longer tradition of ethnic violence, they had important political connotations too. Emphasizing the ethnic, even primordial nature of these wars served more purposes than strictly analytical ones. It offered the opportunity to place the lands of the Caucasus or the Balkans beyond the civilized sphere of contemporary Europe. For many Europeans, ethnic violence in former Yugoslavia was the counter-image of Europe, and could only be interpreted in terms of the 'revenge' or the 'return of history', as excesses of pre-modernity at the borders of post-modern Europe.

In this book, the political dimension of nationalism is prioritized over its other features. It stresses the political role and relevance of nationalism, its political content and function, while simultaneously taking account of its other dimensions. It is not implied that nationalism is either limited to the political realm, that it is purely 'functional', or that it is exclusively and in all respects 'modern'. For the purpose of this book, the definition which understands nationalism as a form of politics explains why the relatively uncontroversial *Lieux de Mémoire* ('places of remembrance') project in France [129] will not be examined, but the German *Historikerstreit*, an aspect of the wider discussion on the essence of German national history and identity and the direction of its (foreign) policies, will be discussed at some length. Little will be found in these pages on Basque folklore and other cultural, artistic, and anthropological aspects of the supposed Basque national identity and nationalism, but the consequences of the armed struggle by the Euskadi Ta Askatasuna (ETA, Basque Country and Freedom) will be debated.

Further readings

The number of studies on nationality and nationalism is vast, and still growing. Only a fraction of the available literature can be mentioned here. For the sake of clarity, a distinction will be made between three categories of studies: the studies on nationalism that are particularly relevant to post-war Europe, the most important comparative and case studies on post-war nationalism, and those general studies of contemporary European history that offer an insight into the historical context of the post-war development of nationalism and nationalist thought.

This introductory chapter began by quoting from John Breuilly's book on nationalism as a form of politics. His *Nationalism and the State* (1982, 1993) still stands out as one of the major studies on nationalism as a distinguishing feature of European politics during the nineteenth and twentieth centuries. Among the other prominent studies of nationalism, one may distinguish between the classical texts that were published during the earlier post-war decades and major general studies of a more recent date. Some of these standard publications have already been mentioned: Hans Kohn's *The Idea of Nationalism* (1944), *Nations and Nationalism* (1983) by Ernest Gellner, *Imagined Communities* (1983, 1993) by Benedict Anderson, and Eric Hobsbawm's *Nations and Nationalism since 1780* (1990).

Recent years have seen a major advance in nationalism research. Every selection is necessarily arbitrary, but the following publications are particularly informative. Malcolm Anderson's *States and Nationalism in Europe since 1945* offers a concise introduction to post-war nationalism, but it ends in the 1990s. Rogers Brubaker's *Citizenship and Nationhood in France and Germany* (1992) and *Nationhood Reframed: Nationhood and the National Question in the New Europe* (1996) cover both Western and (post-)communist Eastern Europe. Yitzhak Brudny gives a unique explanation of cultural nationalism with clear political connotations in late communist Russia in *Reinventing Russia* (1998). Marlène Laruelle's *In the Name of the Nation* (2010) offers the best comprehensive analysis of political nationalism in post-communist Russia. *Ethnonationalism: The Quest for Understanding* (1994) contains an important collection of essays by Walker Connor, who kept the academic interest in ethnic nationalism alive. And among the many studies by Anthony Smith, *Nationalism: Theory, Ideology, History* (2010) deserves special mention as a clear and concise general introduction. Noteworthy are also his *Nationalism in the Twentieth Century* (1979) and *National Identity* (1991). Peter Zwick's *National Communism* (1983) is an early, informative study on how 'national' communist regimes actually were. Claire Sutherland's *Nationalism in the Twenty-First Century* (2012) and Craig Calhoun's *Nations Matter* (2007) primarily discuss the theoretical dimensions of nationalism and national identity. Finally, *The Sage Handbook of Nations and Nationalism* by Gerard Delanty and Krishan Kumar (2006) is unparalleled in scope.

Particularly noteworthy among the collective works on post–Cold War nationalism, containing both theoretical and country case studies, are *Nationalism and Internationalism in the Post-Cold War Era* (2000) by Kjell Goldmann, Ulf Hannerz, and Charles Westin, as well as John A. Hall's *The State of the Nation* (2000), Brian Jenkins and Spyros Sofos's *Nation & Identity in Contemporary Europe* (1996), Ireneusz Karolewski and Andrzej Suszycki's *The Nation and Nationalism in Europe* (2011), and Heinrich August Winkler and Hartmut Kaelble's *Nationalismus – Nationalitäten – Supranationalität* (1993). *Repenser le nationalisme*, edited by Alain Dieckhoff and Christophe Jaffrelot (2006), offers a state-of-the-art overview of French historiography of nationalism.

Although no general or comprehensive history of nationalism or nationalist thought in twentieth-century Europe has been written yet, nationalism figures prominently in multiple studies on political ideas and ideologies in post-war Europe as well as in general histories of the continent. Karl Dietrich Bracher discusses nationalism in *Zeit der Ideologien. Eine Geschichte politischen Denkens im 20. Jahrhundert* (1982). Carsten Holbraad offers a comparable analysis, albeit from a more contemporary perspective, in *Internationalism and Nationalism in European Political Thought* (2003), and so does Neil O'Sullivan in *European Political Thought since 1945* (2004).

There are many excellent studies on the history of post-war Europe that offer the necessary background and context to nationalism. Tony Judt's *Postwar* (2005) is incomparable in scope and depth. It is not without specific biases though, of which Judt's rather uncritical discussion of European integration is probably the most relevant one. Other excellent histories of Europe are *Dark Continent* (1999) by Mark Mazower, which covers the whole twentieth century, especially focusing on the tortuous road of democracy, and *Barbarism and Civilization* (2007) by Bernard Wasserstein. Klaus Larres' *A Companion to Europe since 1945* (2013) contains excellent contributions on themes relevant to contemporary European history, including nationalism. Andreas Wirsching's *Der Preis der Freiheit* (2012) and *Geschichte des Westens* by Heinrich August Winkler (2015) are among the best general histories of Europe after the Cold War. *The European Rescue of the Nation State* (2000) by Alan Milward and *The Choice for Europe* (1998) by Andrew Moravcsik are major studies on European integration, from which important empirical and theoretical conclusions on the role and relevance of the national state, and indirectly on national identity and nationalism, can be inferred.

Most studies on nationalism have a clear normative dimension, but some studies are purposively 'political', without losing their academic value. Michael Billig's *Banal Nationalism* (1995) is an empirical study on everyday 'nationalism', in combination with a convincing argument in favour of a stronger cultural, national foundation of liberal democratic politics. Related studies are *Liberal Nationalism* (1993) by Yael Tamir, and *Nationalism and the Moral Psychology of Community* (2012) by Bernard Yack.

Many of the events that are discussed this book can actually be seen in action on the Internet, especially on YouTube. One can hear de Gaulle solemnly promising his compatriots in December 1958 that overseas Algeria will always remain part of France, slightly over two years before he agreed to the independence of the overseas territory. A visibly nervous Slobodan Milošević of Serbia is seen in April 1987 assuring his fellow Serbs that they will never be beaten again by their Kosovar neighbours. It was one of the opening salvos of the Yugoslav civil wars. And also, Angela Merkel confirming in 2010 before an enthusiastic crowd of party youngsters that multiculturalism has failed completely can be listened to on the Net. It is a great added advantage that the Internet offers to students of contemporary history: one can actually see, witness, what one reads.

2 Europe during the Cold War

European integration[1] and transatlantic cooperation

For the evolution of nations and nationalisms in post-war Europe, the importance of European integration can hardly be overestimated. The advance of European cooperation is among the most historic changes on the continent, and few other developments would impact one another as the national issue and the process of integration did. The first steps towards European cooperation were largely inspired by the urgent desire to tame nationalism, and to strip it of its destructive political influence. This was generally seen as a precondition for cooperation and economic revival. State-driven nationalism was commonly blamed for the political instability and the rise of totalitarianism during the interwar period and for the horrors of the Second World War. It was precisely the European outsider Winston Churchill, the wartime leader of Great Britain, who immediately following the end of the Second World War publicly advocated Franco-German rapprochement as the core of future European cooperation. 'I am ... going to say something that will astonish you', he told an audience in Zurich in September 1946. 'The first step in the re-creation of the European Family must be a partnership between France and Germany. In this way only can France recover the moral and cultural leadership of Europe. There can be no revival of Europe without a spiritually great France and a spiritually great Germany' [29].

---

[1] The process of European integration has developed under different names and abbreviations. What began in 1951 as the European Community for Coal and Steel (ECCS) (Treaty of Paris), would become the European Economic Community in 1957 (Treaty of Rome), and the European Union in 1992 (Maastricht Treaty).

Churchill planned for the United Kingdom to stay outside the 'United States of Europe'. There was nothing wrong with European integration, he alleged, as long as Britain could keep her distance. This view was commonly held across the political board in London for many years after the war. It was not considered to be in the best interests of the United Kingdom to partake in initiatives towards European integration. British national interest was still tightly interwoven with the Empire, and therefore considered difficult to reconcile with the integration of the European states. The economy of the United Kingdom was also more strongly interlinked with the world economy than those of other major European states. Britain carefully cherished its ties with the Commonwealth, as well as its perceived special relationship with the United States. But most importantly perhaps, the British feared that in the process of European integration, Britain would lose its apparently unique character and independence as a nation and as a state. It would lose its national *identity*. In comparison, the geopolitical and economic situation of France, the second major power in Europe, and a colonial power too, was fundamentally different. Although France came out of the war as one of the four Allied victors, defeat, occupation and collaboration had traumatized French society and its political elite. Economically, France was still primarily an agrarian country, and was therefore much more focused on the European market than Great Britain was. France's major geopolitical concern was not to maintain close relations with the United States, but rather to contain Germany through European cooperation under French leadership [184].

The integration of Europe is based on a complex combination of ideals and political calculation, coming together under very specific geopolitical circumstances. European integration was ultimately made possible by conditions that went far beyond Europe's influence. The geopolitical stability of the Western part of Europe, facilitated by the continent's division and guaranteed by the security umbrella of the transatlantic alliance, enabled the Benelux countries, Italy, France and Germany to take the first steps in the integration process, from the late 1940s. The Cold War provided an ideal context for European integration, in Western Europe and, albeit under very dissimilar conditions and in a different form, in the Eastern part of the continent. Europe needed outside powers to start the integration process. Cooperation was inspired by

Europe's weakness and insecurity, rather than by its strength or self-confidence. 'So long as Europe was the metropolis of world power, the unilateralism, the ambitions, of nation states left no room for a marriage of reason', writes François Duchêne, journalist and biographer of Jean Monnet. It was the deplorable situation after the war, when 'all the founding states of the Community ... had been defeated and shaken to their moral and material foundations', that made European integration possible [43: 404–5]. So without direct British involvement but with firm American support, Europeans took the first institutional steps towards cooperation. On the initiative of Jean Monnet, the founding father of European integration whom Duchêne so elegantly characterized as 'the first statesman of interdependence', six countries agreed on the 'Schuman Plan', named after the Minister of Foreign Affairs of France, Robert Schuman (1948–52). The Schuman Plan envisaged a common, 'High Authority' over French and German coal and steel production. In April 1951, France, Germany, Italy and the three Benelux countries, Belgium, Luxembourg and, after some hesitation, especially because of the absence of the United Kingdom, the Netherlands, signed the Treaty of Paris, which founded the European Coal and Steel Community (ECSC).

The ECSC came into force in July 1952. Monnet, who in a manner typical of the technocratic nature of European cooperation had never held any major political function, became its first president (1952–6). The choice to integrate steel and coal markets was logical. These were the most important strategic industries in Europe, at the basis of national military power, and conditional for the revival of Western European industry. Monnet, Schuman and German Chancellor Konrad Adenauer (1949–63) were the driving forces behind Franco-German rapprochement and the initial phase of European integration. The ECSC proved a political and economic success, aptly combining the partly divergent interests of France and Germany, as well as the common cause of European cooperation. The ECSC facilitated Germany's comeback onto the European political stage and it served the French interest to co-exercise control over a crucial industry in a strategic region, the Ruhr. Tony Judt [87: 156] aptly characterized the ECSC as a European solution to a French national problem.

Five years later, in March 1957, the same six countries that had taken the initiative to create the ECSC signed the Treaty of Rome, thereby establishing the European Community, the forerunner of the European Union. The Treaty of Rome was greeted with enthusiasm in Germany, Italy and the Low Countries (with the communist parties as the main dissidents), but received with a considerable dose of scepticism in France. From his self-imposed political exile in Colombey-les-Deux-Églises, France's former wartime leader Charles de Gaulle spoke out against the agreement. It was thanks to the socialist party that the French parliament ratified it. On 1 January 1958, the Treaty of Rome came into force.

The process of European cooperation was typified by the signatories of the Treaty of Rome as an 'ever closer union among the European peoples' [171]. In reality, cooperation in Europe followed a slow and zigzag course, a pattern of progress, stagnation, crisis and progress again. European integration was a leap into the unknown. It did not start from an optimistic, confident idea of the future, but rather from a severe disillusionment with the recent past, and a sense of insecurity among the West European nations. From the very start, it was an uncertain political process between individual, sovereign national states, each with their own interests and identities, which advanced with difficulties, in fits and starts. Periods of great activity, enthusiasm and progress in the early 1950s and the 1990s were interspersed with moments of obvious stagnation and even failure, such as the early rejection by the French parliament of the European Defence Community (EDC) in August 1954. The historian Bernard Wasserstein reminds us of how the French parliamentarians, after they voted down the EDC, rose and raised in triumph the Marseillaise [175: 457] – the French national interest had prevailed.

In 1973, after long negotiations and embarrassing hesitations, the United Kingdom finally joined the European Community, together with Ireland and Denmark. Despite the evident political importance of the accession of the United Kingdom, the practical relevance was mainly economic as one of Europe's largest economies was added to the internal market. Consecutive rounds of enlargement were primarily driven by political motives. In 1981 and 1986, the former dictatorships Greece, Spain and Portugal joined the Union. In comparison, the accession of Austria, Finland and Sweden on 1 January 1995 went almost unnoticed. Their membership was especially economically motivated again. A fourth country, Norway, abstained from joining the Union. Following on from these developments, the largest expansion in the history of the European Union took place after the Cold War, in 2004. Eight former communist countries, Poland, the Czech Republic, Estonia, Latvia, Lithuania, Hungary, Slovakia and Slovenia, plus Greek Cyprus and Malta joined the Union. They were followed in 2007 by Bulgaria and Romania (Croatia joined in 2013). The Cold War was finally over, Europe was no longer institutionally divided and the European Union had changed radically.

The diversity and continued relevance of Europe's member states are echoed in scholarly interpretations of the development of European integration. 'The tension between the nation-state and international integration is central to any discussion of the development of the European political system', as the British political scientist William Wallace [174: 21–2] put it. The debate begins with the assessment of how and why the founding members decided to start the integration process at all. For sure, there was an element of idealism involved. European integration partly stemmed from the shared ambition to deal with the continent's dramatic recent past of nationalism and rivalry between states. European integration offered an escape from the reality of the failed nation state (*'aus dem gescheiterten Nationalstaat'*) [88: 192]. From this perspective, Europe cooperation was envisaged as an initiative aimed against the traditional ambitions of national states to maximize their powers at the expense of others. From another perspective, however, European integration was precisely meant to facilitate the member states' continuance of their traditional role and to maintain their significance [122]. One can indeed safely assume that none of the national governments that took the initiative to cooperate, nor any of the states that would join the Union later, acted in the belief that they would be marginalized in the process. Rather, the opposite was true. European integration was understood as a mechanism that would give states the opportunity to better perform their traditional tasks, national security and the well-being of their citizens, not against but in cooperation with their neighbours. The actual impact of European cooperation on the role and significance of the national state remains controversial. One could argue convincingly that European cooperation has set significant limits to the sovereignty and to the capacity to act independently of the national state. But with equal persuasion one could assert that European integration actually offered member states the unique opportunity to enhance their capabilities through partially pooling them.

The federalist aspirations of Jean Monnet and his contemporaries have not had a lasting impact on the scholarly debate on European cooperation and the national state. Early debates were dominated by the belief that integration was largely driven by its own logic, by the logic of functionalism. The American political scientist Ernst Haas [65] popularized the idea that European integration was shaped by a 'spillover effect': integration in one area created pressure for further cooperation in other realms. Haas's neo-functionalism nuanced both the relevance of federalist ideas and the role of the national states. It gave the process of institutional cooperation the appearance of being logical and almost inevitable.

Haas would later revise his functionalist approach. His intellectual turn was particularly inspired by de Gaulle's continuing national assertiveness, symbolic of the sustained influence of national governments on the pace and direction of integration. More researchers now emphasized the enduring influence and significance of the nation state in Europe. European integration should be considered as a 'normal' form of international relations that gave no specific reason to believe that it would either weaken the national state or lead to any kind of supranational community [70; 71]. The British economic historian Alan Milward came to such a conclusion, albeit from a different perspective. All supranational rhetoric notwithstanding, European cooperation had been realized under the full control of its members, Milward argued – member states whose independence and sovereignty it had strengthened rather than compromised. European integration had a positive impact on the effectiveness and the legitimacy of the national states. The primacy of, and the loyalty to, the nation state was strengthened, not weakened through the process. European integration had been an integral part of the 'reassertion of the nation-state as an organizational concept', as Milward concluded. Europe had 'rescued' the nation state [122: 2–3]. Milward's critique of the neo-functionalist approach would have a lasting influence on the historiography of European integration. The American political scientist Andrew Moravcsik [123] defined the member states' commercial interests as the prime motivation for European integration. His liberal intergovernmentalist approach argued that integration had always remained a matter of rational, interest-driven cooperation between fully sovereign national governments. European integration advanced when these national commercial interests converged, and stalled when they fundamentally conflicted.

Recent scholarship on European integration continues to agree on the lasting relevance of the national state, although not without important qualifications. Influenced by the new dynamics and further deepening of the integration processes from the early 1990s, scholars came to see 'Europe' as a novel, a unique 'political system'. The distinction between this international system and the national member states became increasingly obscure. National states remained crucially important actors in the integration process, but they could no longer be isolated from the system as a whole. The European Union had become a complex form of 'multi-level governance' [148].

Although European cooperation certainly created a dynamic of its own, and what has been achieved cannot only be explained by the almost exclusively economic rationalism *à la* Milward and Moravcsik, in essence the process of integration has always been a matter of intergovernmental cooperation. The calculating behaviour of national governments was at the basis of the initiation, the deepening and the widening of European integration. For France, extensive cooperation with neighbouring states offered an ideal opportunity to prevent either a renewed increase in military power or another *Alleingang* by Germany. European cooperation would include Germany in a new European order, partly under French control, and in cooperation with, though not subordinated to, the United States. For the Federal Republic of Germany, the reverse could be argued. European integration and transatlantic cooperation paved the way for international acceptance and legitimacy as a civilized nation and a reliable ally, and it held the door open for future reunification. 'The turn towards Europe for many Germans was an attempt to escape from their own national past' [147: 329]. So, paradoxically, the frameworks of European integration and transatlantic cooperation actually gave Germany foreign policy room to manoeuvre. They would continue to define the parameters of its international relations from the early years of the Cold War into the 1990s, when the geopolitical situation changed fundamentally and would allow the two Germanies to reunite. The geopolitical considerations of France and Germany have proved remarkably resilient, during and also after the Cold War.

For the member states of 'Europe', their political elites and their generally not particularly interested citizens, European integration did not conflict with the national interest. The one supposedly served the other, and vice versa. But despite the fact that the perceived interests of the nation states motivated and guided the integration process, European integration and transatlantic cooperation have also been disputed, and often from nationalist positions. Opposition against the transatlantic alliance was mostly inspired by political concerns over US foreign and security policies, including such rallying issues as the war in Vietnam during the 1960s. But there was often an element of national or cultural anti-Americanism involved too. Cultural anti-Americanism in Western Europe had strong elitist and intellectual features. 'Anti-Americanism was markedly less pronounced lower down the social scale among those enjoying the new popular cultures than among the intellectuals and defenders of the old high culture', as the historian Mark Mazower concludes for most of the post-war era [117: 309]. Cultural anti-Americanism was not related to any particular political persuasion. The left and right occasionally critiqued the expansionism of the 'American way of life' and its undermining impact on the interests and the identity of one's own nation. Political anti-Americanism on the other hand tended to be less 'nationally' coloured and more politically and ideologically inspired. Very vocal minorities often loudly expressed their opposition against US foreign policies, but overall with relatively little long-term effect. No single Western European government has ever seriously reconsidered its country's alliance with the United States. France is the exception that again proves the rule. Cultural and political anti-Americanism in France were intimately linked, especially during de Gaulle's presidential terms. Additionally, French anti-Americanism has always had strongly national, if not nationalist, features. Aversion to the power and influence of the United States, and to the type of society it represented, expressed itself in many ways, from verbal and sometimes physical hostility to the presence of American fast-food restaurants and marketing icons such as Coca-Cola and Hollywood movies, to the exit by France from the military structures of the North Atlantic Treaty Organization (NATO) and the tenacious opposition to EC membership of the United Kingdom, the alleged outpost of the United States in Europe [12].

Opposition to European integration was also based on a combination of ideological and political arguments, although probably more nationally inspired than anti-Americanism. The political belief that 'Europe' was really a tool of big business' interests was traditionally an argument of left-wing parties, but eventually spread also to more conservative populist parties. This notion should be distinguished from the much more widespread and fairly resilient view that European integration was too 'liberal', too much focused on economic and monetary issues only. Generally, however, Euroscepticism, that is serious political concerns about the actual process of cooperation in Europe, has typically been inspired by the rather indistinct idea that European integration harmed national interests and the identity of the member state. In different ways and for mostly dissimilar reasons, especially France and Britain have reflected an ambivalent attitude towards the relationship between European cooperation and their alleged national interests during the course of European integration.

General de Gaulle had little doubt: European integration served the national interest of France, but only as long as it would remain subordinate to it. This is a perfect illustration of the ambiguous relationship between European integration and nationalism. Nationalism can be for and against deeper European corporation. It depends on the context. And the context in this case is the extent to which France would be able to dominate the process of European integration, including the embedding of Germany within the Community. As one of the founders of European cooperation, France contributed more than any other member state to the institutional development of the integration process. Europe's bureaucratic *mentalité* was always very French. This however did not stop de Gaulle, after his return to the presidency in January 1959, from opposing what he considered as the supranational direction into which the other members, Germany in particular, had led the Community. The French president was vehemently opposed to suggestions to limit the national veto in Commission decision-making. In July 1965, de Gaulle prohibited French ministers from further participating in the meetings of the European Council, thereby effectively frustrating the decision-making process in Brussels. The so-called 'empty chair crisis' kept the community paralysed for more than six months. The compromise that the president of the Commission, Walter Hallstein (1958–67), would eventually secure shifted the political initiative back again from the Commission to the member states.

Shortly after the empty chair crisis, de Gaulle announced another unilateral French decision, to leave the integrated military command of NATO. NATO bases in the country were to close their doors, and its military command centre, Supreme Headquarters Allied Powers Europe (SHAPE), was expelled from Paris and moved to Bergen, in Belgium. Armed with its nuclear *force de frappe*, France aspired to sail an independent course, together with Europe but under French guidance. Although secret military contacts with the alliance were restored within a year after France's exit, it would take until April 2009 before France became a fully fledged member state of NATO again. 'De Gaulle's nationalism was motivated by a concern for national sovereignty, and ultimately for the survival of France as a great power' [72: 107]. De Gaulle's nationalism went hand in hand with a conservative internationalism whose political purpose was to construct a Europe that, stretching from the Atlantic to the Urals, and under the direction of France in the West, would be strong enough to counterbalance the power of the United States.

An important element of de Gaulle's geopolitical calculation was to keep the United Kingdom out of the European Community. De Gaulle considered London to be Washington's 'Trojan horse' in Europe. Twice he voiced his *non* against accession of the country, in January 1963 and again in November 1967 – to the satisfaction of many British Eurosceptics and to the despair of the British government. For its part, the United States, which at that time was as much in favour of British membership as it would be of the integration of Turkey in later decades, firmly rejected the French position. Initially, France's obstinate attitude had garnered the sympathy of other member states. They also considered the British preference for a free-trade zone rather than a deeper community to be outdated. As time passed, however, de Gaulle's stubborn position aroused anger and frustration. Among other member states, British involvement became increasingly perceived as a welcome counterweight against French domination. But de Gaulle persisted, and only his successor, Georges Pompidou (1969–74), surrendered France's opposition to the accession of the United Kingdom. Pompidou was motivated by the very same French national interests, which he however interpreted differently. He expected that the inclusion of a country with an economy as large and a public opinion as reserved as Great Britain's would help to counterbalance the growing economic weight of Germany as well as the supranational tendencies within the Community. Pompidou may in fact have been more prognostic than his illustrious predecessor.

Within or without Europe, the British have never been particularly enthusiastic about the process of integration. It was commonly felt, and not without reason, that accession to the European Community would symbolize and effectuate the end of the status of Britain as a world power. Eventual accession to the Community was primarily motivated by economic reasons, but it would remain more controversial than in any other member state. Still in 1983, the Labour Party had entered the general elections promising to withdraw from Europe. The United Kingdom would generally take cautious positions in most realms of integration. Prime Minister Margaret Thatcher (1979–90), British Conservative and Eurosceptic European, kept her foot down until she was able to secure a significant rebate, to compensate for the country's net contribution to the European budget. The British government negotiated a special position on the Economic and Monetary Union, the Schengen Agreement, and several other aspects of integration in the field of justice, social policy and home affairs. Britain's Euroscepticism has never been strictly party related, and neither were its pro-European sentiments. Prime Minister Edward Heath (1970–4) was a Conservative who would steer his country into the European Community, while Thatcher's Labour successor Prime Minister Tony Blair (1997–2007) was widely seen as the most enthusiastic European who had ever moved into No. 10 Downing Street.

The reservations of the British were mirrored by the enthusiasm of the Germans. Integration into Europe seemed to perfectly serve the strategic considerations of Germany's first post-war chancellor, the Christian Democrat Konrad Adenauer (1949–63). Integration into Europe allowed him to regain an international reputation, to enhance German foreign policy options and to maintain the longer-term prospect of reunification. The Social Democrats under Kurt Schumacher initially took a considerably more 'nationalist' view. Among Social Democrats, Adenauer was blemished as the 'Chancellor of the Allies', while Schumacher was hailed as the champion of German unity. Schumacher was not against integration in Western Europe, but only as long as it would be based on 'strongly autonomous nation-states' [145: 170], and it would not reduce the chances of German reunification. He initially pleaded for a neutralist foreign policy, rather than a pro-Western one. The Social Democrat was driven by pragmatic more than ideological concerns. He attached priority, at least in public, to the prospect of German unification over the possibility of European integration. Otherwise, Schumacher was a convinced anti-communist. He distrusted the Soviets and their East German allies deeply.

A critical part of the German population, and certainly its political elite, would continue to see Germany's anchoring in Europe as a precondition for German unification. They proved right. It would take a fundamental change of Europe's geopolitical reality, the end of the Cold War, to put the issue of German unification firmly on the agenda. *Wir sind das Volk!* the opposition in the German Democratic Republic (GDR) chanted during the final weeks of the communist regime, in the fall of 1989 – 'We are the people!' Once the communist dictatorship had fallen, many East Germans called for early unification: 'We are *one* people!' *Wir sind ein Volk!* Hundreds of thousands of East German citizens had already left their country for West Germany in the months before and after the Berlin Wall had opened, unexpectedly and accidentally, on the night of 8–9 November 1989.

With varying degrees of enthusiasm, the leaders of the two great powers, US President George H. W. Bush (1989–93) and Soviet party leader and President Mikhail Gorbachev (1985–91) accepted the reunification of Germany. Gorbachev had long insisted on the continuation of the division of Germany and on the sovereignty of the German Democratic Republic, but he eventually agreed to unification, under the impact of the rapid and ultimately irreversible course of events in the Eastern part of Europe, as well as of the tens of billions of Deutschmarks the government in Bonn promised to earmark for the economic reconstruction of the Soviet Union and its successor states. But Gorbachev was not alone in his reservations. The French President François Mitterrand (1981–95), the British Prime Minister Margaret Thatcher (1979–90), her Dutch colleague Ruud Lubbers (1982–94) and even the first post-communist leadership in Poland – so, most of Germany's neighbours – showed their misgivings about the rapid geopolitical changes in the very heart of Europe. Germany's Chancellor Helmut Kohl (1982–98) irritably dismissed these concerns, and his major argument was indeed the firm anchoring of Germany in an integrated Europe and a transatlantic alliance. German reunification was another illustration of the diverse relation between the 'national' and the 'international' in post-war European history, different in nature but not in substance from how de Gaulle had used international cooperation to serve the national interest. The reunion of the two German states essentially meant the full incorporation of the GDR into the Federal Republic. Notwithstanding the frustration and the anger many East Germans felt over the arrogant way they were occasionally treated by the *Besserwessis* (a contraction of 'Westerners who know better') and about their new and often uncertain living conditions, including unemployment, the legitimacy of reunification was disputed by very few Germans from the eastern *Länder*. Any typically East German or GDR national identity had proved ephemeral at most. And if there were any deeper feelings of nostalgia for socialism in the former GDR, they remained mostly limited to the folklore of *petit bourgeois* 'welfarism', so brilliantly portrayed in the award-winning German film *Goodbye, Lenin!* (2003).

Was nationalism important in the process towards German reunification? Breuilly answers the question negatively [17: 354]. There was no oppositionist movement in the GDR, before or after the fall of the wall, that sought power on the basis of the national ideal. Basically all efforts by the communist leadership in East Germany to foster a genuine GDR national identity or sense of nationality had proven ineffective. As for the West German government, it had only pushed for unification once the breakdown of the East German communist regime (and economy) had become evident and irreversible, and the international environment, especially the political support of the US administration and the acquiescence of the Russian leadership, had been secured.

The 'national idea' had remained present in the two German states throughout the post-war era, albeit in rather different guises. With only minor exceptions however did it ever develop into anything radically nationalist. Reunification never ceased to be a formal objective of West German governments, irrespective of their political colouring. The ambition of reunification was even enshrined in Germany's constitution. As the years passed, however, the prospect of reunion disappeared from sight. Regional integration projects in the East and West of Europe and a range of international agreements had given the division of Germany a strong sense of permanence. The reality of the two German states increasingly prevailed over the ever-weaker notion of one German nation. The large majority of East Germans probably never expected to ever see the reunion with the West of Germany. But when the occasion arose in the late 1980s, they supported it wholeheartedly, if not out of a deeper felt sense of shared German identity, then out of a desire to join a clearly more powerful and wealthy neighbour. Many West Germans may have had more reservations about the timing and the speed of the reunification, but they also shared the ambition. Dissident voices were relatively few at both sides of the inner-German border. They mainly expressed concern over the foreign policy consequences of an enlarged and more powerful Germany. The reunification of Germany may have been inspired and motivated by a persistent 'national idea', but it could only be successful because of other circumstantial factors, especially the breakdown of the East German communist party state and a permissive international environment.

Generally, nationalism in its many variations had been strongly disqualified in post-war German politics from immediately after the Second World War. *Stunde Null*, as the moment of Germany's unconditional surrender and collapse in 1945 was dubbed, may not have brought the full and definite break with its totalitarian past, but nationalism had largely lost its legitimizing purpose. It no longer had the moral foundation needed for an integrative ideology [178: 12]. And different from what sceptics of the *deutsche Einheit* had anticipated, the political significance of national identity or nationalism in Germany did not fundamentally change after reunification either. In a united Germany, nationalism did not represent a fundamentally more powerful basis of political identity or legitimacy than it had in the two separate German states. What mostly changed was Germany's international position and, to a certain extent, its foreign policies. These became more autonomous, and more assertive. Whether this should be interpreted as one of 'the effects of German nationalism at the supranational level' [93: 127] remains questionable. For the large power which Germany is, its foreign and security policies remained cautious, moderate, and evidently pro-European, throughout the first post–Cold War decades.

Changing the concept of the 'national': decolonization and the welfare state

The second half of the twentieth century was a time of unprecedented historical change. Some developments were eventually turned back, such as the Cold War division of the continent and the expansion of the Soviet Union, but other changes remained permanent. Two of these historical changes deserve to be discussed at a certain length: decolonization and the welfare state. While the dismantling of Europe's colonial empires and the building of the welfare state were distinct, non-related phenomena, they would both have a great impact on the states and nations of Europe, initially especially in Western Europe but later also in the Eastern part of the continent, and, as far as decolonization is concerned, especially in Russia after the dissolution of the Soviet Union. Decolonization and the welfare state would deeply affect the concept of the 'national' in Europe. They would change the composition of society, the relationship between the state and society and the role and relevance, including the (self-)understanding, of the nation. The dismantling of Europe's colonial empires ended the perception and the reality of Europe's major states as global powers and it triggered a migration movement into Europe, which would significantly change the composition of the nations involved. The building of the welfare state would have a different but comparably important impact on the nation and the nation state in Europe. It considerably expanded the tasks and responsibilities of the state and it added profoundly new, socio-economic privileges to citizenship.

The dismantling of its overseas colonies was one of post-war Europe's irreversible historical changes. In a few decades, all of the colonial empires crumbled, with the exception of the Soviet empire. The Soviet Union did not formally cease to exist until December 1991. And even insofar as the successor state to the Soviet Union, the Russian Federation, can be understood as a nation state, it remained one with strong 'imperial' characteristics, with a very diverse population, and a series of rebellious areas in its periphery, especially in the Caucasus.

Anti-colonialism is an important variant of nationalism and a prominent trajectory in nationalism research. It was especially, perhaps only, in the context of decolonization that nationalism continued to be seen by many Europeans as progressive and liberalizing.

Nationalism and national sovereignty were among Europe's most successful exports to the rest of the world [116: 111], including the new states of Africa and Asia. The focus of academic study is still mostly on the role and relevance of nationalist thought and action in colonial territories and post-colonial countries, and the transformative effects these had on global politics. The impact of decolonization on the colonizing powers has received less attention, despite the fact that for many countries few other events changed the shape of the state and ultimately also the nation more permanently than decolonization. The post-war withdrawal of European powers from their colonial possessions reduced their global role and critically changed the geopolitical map of the world. Additionally, decolonization would trigger multiple waves of immigration, which not only altered the composition of metropolitan society, but also transformed the idea of what being a 'Dutchman', a 'Frenchman' or even a 'European' meant [39: 113].

After the Second World War, the legitimation of colonial rule became increasingly problematic. Traditional arguments as the spread of civilization, religion or responsible governance were no longer convincing. Containment of communist expansion as an argument for the continuation of overseas rule sounded more plausible, but did not work either. Anti-communism was not ideally served by the continuation of colonial relations. Colonialism actually strengthened the appeal of communism in Africa and Asia, and it promoted the international standing of the Soviet Union, the major self-proclaimed global anti-imperialist power. This eventually left just one convincing motive for the continuation of colonialism: the national interest. '*Indië verloren, rampspoed geboren!*' was a popular slogan in post-war Netherlands: losing the East Indies would be economically disastrous. It remained a largely empty slogan. Not only did it fail to strike a chord beyond the Netherlands, but it also proved false. Decolonization would have little negative impact on the economic development of the Western European powers, the Netherlands included. In contrast to the economic relevance of colonialism, its cultural and geopolitical legacy had a far longer impact. Although the history of modern European imperialism, of the great colonial empires, had been relatively short, colonialism remained as a dominant aspect of modern European political and cultural history, and it remained vital to the identity of many European nations.

Decolonization took place within a brief time span, albeit along very different trajectories and with fierce aftershocks. For Britain's main colony India, the experiment with partial self-government paved the way for a reasonably smooth independence. It could not however prevent the subsequent partition of the former Raj into a predominantly Muslim Pakistan and a Hindu India, a partition which was accompanied by massive refugee flows and mutual ethnic and religious violence. British decolonization in Africa also produced ethnic tensions, sparking tribal warfare and political upheaval. The dismantling of the Dutch and French colonial empires and overseas possessions resulted in similar violent outbursts. From 1945 to 1949, Dutch troops fought a colonial war, presented as 'police actions' in the Dutch East Indies (Indonesia). The military operations were not particularly popular in the Netherlands, and they could not count on the support of the country's main ally, the United States. The French colonial adventure in South-East Asia also ended in failure. As embarrassing as the French defeat at Dien Bien Phu (Vietnam, March–May 1954) was, it proved of relatively minor importance in comparison with two other convulsions of French decolonization, the Suez Crisis in 1956 and the struggle for independence in Algeria from the 1950s. The combined Israeli, French and British military operations against Egypt in July 1956, in response to the nationalization of the Suez Canal by the Egyptian President Gamal Nasser (1956–70), ended in a complete political fiasco. Even before the British and French troops had managed to establish full control over the Suez Canal, they were forced to beat a hasty retreat. Under intense political pressure from the Soviet Union, the United Nations and especially the United States, first Britain and then France decided to cease their late colonial adventure. What was meant to strengthen the position of Britain and France in the Near East effectively eliminated their traditional influence in the region, accelerated their imperial decline and refocused their attention on Europe.

Even if the Suez fiasco could still be rationalized away as a shared foreign policy failure, the war of independence that raged from 1954 in the overseas territory of Algeria plunged France into a deep, almost existential crisis. The conflict was fought with great tenacity and ferocity. It divided the French nation, triggered dangerous political violence in metropolitan France and crippled the democratic system of government. Crucially, it also brought Charles de Gaulle back to power. On 21 December 1958, the general was elected as President of the Fifth Republic by a large majority of the electorate. '*Je vous ai compris!*', de Gaulle assured an enthusiastic crowd in Algiers six months before his elections. 'I have got the message': Algeria would remain French forever.

De Gaulle's promise was widely appreciated in France and among the French in Algeria, but, gradually, the general would recognize the unsustainability of French authority over North Africa. To the resentment of the Algerians of French or European origin, the *pieds-noirs* or 'black feet', de Gaulle decided to hold a referendum on the independence of France's overseas territory. He gave his support to negotiations with the main liberation movement, the Front de Libération Nationale (FLN) or National Liberation Front, which would eventually result in the Évian Accords of March 1962, which brought a formal end to the war. De Gaulle was the only leader who combined the power, the prestige and the courage to ultimately reconcile the people of France with the independence of their most precious colonial possession. On 3 July 1962, the president declared Algeria independent. His decision was based on the same consideration, the very same national interest that had before committed him to hold on to colonial rule over northern Africa. 'Decolonization is in our interest', he told his compatriots at a press conference in April 1961; 'decolonization is our policy' (quoted in [151: 199]).

Half a century after the European colonial empires had reached their peak, colonial rule had become history. Europe had given up its global aspirations reluctantly and now had to reinvent itself again. Decolonization was one of those defining moments of the continent in the twentieth century and was a process firmly linked to national identity and European integration. For most colonial powers – smaller ones such as the Netherlands, Belgium and Portugal, but also for the larger ones, Britain and especially France – European integration was partly meant to compensate for the loss of global wealth and prestige after the collapse of empire [70: 118–20].

In parallel with the redrawing of the geopolitical map of the world, and Europe's place within it, other political developments would permanently affect the national states in Western Europe too. Among the most crucial changes were the positive reappraisal of democracy and the establishment of the welfare state. After the first post-war years of chaos, poverty and retribution, the political value of democracy would become almost generally accepted. The first three post-war decades were Europe's 'democratic age' [32: 71] – democratic consensus that was facilitated by almost uninterrupted economic growth. In the early 1960s, the sociologist Daniel Bell famously translated this political consensus into his end-of-ideology thesis. What used to be a powerful 'road to action', Bell concluded about ideology in contemporary European politics, had become 'a dead end' [10: 393]. '[T]here is today a rough consensus among intellectuals on political issues: the acceptance of the Welfare State; the desirability of decentralized power; a system of mixed economy and of political pluralism ... the ideological age has ended' [10: 393, 397].

For the time being, the main challenge to parliamentary democracy came from the left, and, contrary to Bell, it was not devoid of ideological inspiration. The popular communist parties in Italy, France and other countries would only reluctantly accept the democratic order. Communist ideology inspired large minorities of West Europeans until well into the 1970s. Traditional conservative mistrust of democracy found relatively little political support after the war, especially in comparison with the interwar years. It remained mostly hidden in the shadowy sub-world of political intrigues by parts of the military, security and economic elites. Public protests and political violence against the current political order remained exceptional in post-war Europe. But what historians would refer to as a period of remarkable political harmony, many (younger) contemporaries experienced as years of stifling consensus and conformism – their protest would follow in due course.

Post-war economic reconstruction in Western Europe was facilitated by strong state intervention, including economic planning and nationalization on a scale never before seen. It laid the foundation for an essentially novel socio-political construct: the national welfare state. The idea of the welfare state built on initiatives taken in various countries before and during the war. The introduction of old-age pension by German Chancellor Otto von Bismarck (1871–90) is generally seen as one such prototypical measure. The actual forerunner to the welfare state however was the policy of massive state intervention in the economy and society during the war, especially in the United Kingdom. 'The warfare state ... shaped the welfare state' [175: 444].

Welfare during the early years of post-war reconstruction in Europe should not be taken too literally though. Wages generally remained low, and there was little room for social benefits. Only from the late 1960s would the welfare state expand from a limited range of protective measures to a comprehensive package of social benefits and guarantees. 'National governments became giant insurance companies' [121: 14]. The precise nature of the welfare state and the social provisions it delivered varied by country. The Danish sociologist Gøsta Esping-Andersen [44] emphasized the context-specific nature of the welfare state and drew a distinction between three different types: the liberal or Anglo-Saxon model in the United Kingdom; the corporatist model in Austria, France, Germany and Italy; and the social-democratic model in the Scandinavian countries and the Netherlands. All varieties of the welfare state had one important feature in common: they were not only political and socio-economic constructions but also and principally national ones.

The welfare state became a truly national arrangement, serving the interests of societies at large, providing social benefits to the poor, the middle class, and the rest of the population. Practically the entire political spectrum embraced it. The welfare state was as much shaped by Christian democratic parties, the major new political force after the war, as by their social democratic contenders [89]. Still it is social democracy with which the welfare state is mostly closely identified. After the Second World War, the social democratic movement went through a triple process of change and adaptation, which would have important consequences for its position towards the national state and international cooperation [145]. Social democrats dropped most of their remaining reservations against parliamentary democracy; they accepted the market-based economic order; and they would conform to the major international dimensions of post-war reality, European integration and transatlantic cooperation. It took social democracy longer than its liberal and Christian democratic competitors to think beyond the national state. Many social democrats continued to regard European integration as a predominantly liberal exercise, too much focused on market integration only. They would continue to retain their doubts about the EU into the 1980s. By then, however, most parties began to appreciate the European Union as an alternative instrument of political engineering, complementary to the apparently ever less effective national state. Social democracy would develop into perhaps the most pro-European of all major political currents. It became 'the party group of big government in the new Europe' [72: 81], increasingly emphasizing the need to further strengthen the administrative capabilities and the social dimension of the European Union. Conservatives, liberals and even Christian democrats were generally more reserved about the further transfer of prerogatives from the national governments to Brussels.

Nation, state and welfare became increasingly intertwined in Europe. The more expansive welfare states especially were facilitated by a substantial redistribution of the national income. The entitlement to welfare provisions gave an additional relevance to the concept of the nation, and to citizenship. Citizens no longer enjoyed only political rights but had also acquired social privileges. The welfare state contributed significantly to the consolidation of nationality and national identity. As the Swedish economist and Nobel laureate Karl Gunnar Myrdal [127: 185] phrased it, the welfare state strongly enlarged the number of people who felt a 'belonging' to the nation. The welfare state was designed to function as a 'closed' arrangement, limited to the citizens of a given state and lawfully discriminating against those of others. Yet another important national effect of the growing number of welfare provisions was the expansion of the state's responsibilities and of the bureaucracy that would deliver these goods. The nation state 'is everywhere becoming stronger', Myrdal wrote in 1960, not without regrets. He criticized the welfare state as overly protectionist and nationalistic. National integration is realized at the expense of international cooperation, he argued [127: 155, 159, 162]. The welfare state as built during the first three post-war decades represented the 'culmination of the nation-state' [110: 133].

The *Trente Glorieuses*, as these first post-war decades of almost uninterrupted economic expansion are referred to in France, would last until the global oil crisis of the early 1970s. The sudden and drastic price hike marked the beginning of a period of economic stagnation, social discontent and political turmoil, which would continue into the next decade. Full employment, one of the core aspects of the earlier decades, was over, and as yet not to return again. Initially in the United States and with a certain delay in Western Europe too, job losses in traditional industry would change the face of modern society. The icon of the era of modern industrial society, the unionized, white, male, single-wage earner, gradually faded away. Most European economies continued to grow, albeit slowly and hesitantly, but the zeitgeist became less optimistic, even sombre. The late 1970s and early 1980s were the time of 'doom and gloom', of 'the lost generation'. 'In the life of the mind, the 1970s were the most dispirited decade of the twentieth century', wrote Judt. Europe's 'good times' were over. '[T]he Seventies were an age of cynicism, of lost illusions and reduced expectations' [87: 477–8]. This traditionally poor image of the decade, of a depressing intermezzo between the cheerful 1960s and the dynamic 1980s, has only recently been revised. Historians have reinterpreted the 1970s as a hinge moment that dramatically changed and durably transformed Western society. The simultaneous spread of the two great, partly contradictory undercurrents of egalitarianism and free-market economics would actually reshape the world. The global 1970s were a decade of poor reputation, but great importance [14: 3–4].

Due to the early crisis and the later changes of the 1970s, the welfare state came under increasing pressure too. The promise of liberalism and the free market (the *laissez-faire* approach) gradually supplanted the Keynesian orthodoxy of monetary and fiscal government and high public spending. US President Ronald Reagan (1981–9) and the British Prime Minister Margaret Thatcher paved the way for a global neoliberal economic reorientation [133]. Still, the welfare state survived as one of the most resilient aspects of the post-war order in Europe. Over the course of the years, it may have been adapted and downsized, critiqued and vilified, but it has never lost its societal or political legitimacy, also, if not mainly, because of its typically *national* character.

Daniel Bell [10] believed that during the 1960s, the Western world, and Europe in particular, had not only entered a post-ideological phase but also, especially due to the process of European integration, a post-national era. We now know that both inferences were premature. The social and political changes that occurred from the end of the 1960s may not have been heavily ideologically inspired, but they did signify an end to the social consensus and conformism that was typical of the first post-war decades. The role of nationalism in the wave of political unrest is little observed. The protests by young people, especially students, against the old political and socio-economic order are generally considered as a typically transnational phenomenon, and indeed, in organization and inspiration, the student protests had strong international and cross-border features. The first student protests, however, which took place in May 1966, at Leuven University, Belgium, were actually triggered by specifically nationalist concerns, linked with Belgium's intractable nationalities' issue. Flemish students demonstrated against the continuing presence of their francophone colleagues on the Flemish campus after the university had been officially divided into a Flemish and a Wallonian or French-speaking chapter. *Walen buiten*, 'Wallonians Out', was the very first slogan of the student revolt during the late 1960s. The students' demands in Leuven changed rapidly though, and quickly acquired a more anti-clerical, anti-establishment and internationalist nature. Already by November 1967, student leaders came together in Paris to discuss what they considered as their foremost problem: common student apathy [76: 1]. When in March the following year a busload of by-then-hardened Belgian student activists left for the French capital again, apathy was long gone. Activists easily moved across borders. Motivated by the civil rights movement and opposition to the war in Vietnam on the campuses of American universities, students in Italy, Germany and France emerged onto the streets. Their goals were as vehemently expressed as they were incoherently defined, to paraphrase Wasserstein:

> In spite of the effervescence of colourful groupuscules of Trotskyists, Maoists, and anarchists, most participants were mobilized less by ideology than by a vague sense of generational solidarity against an establishment seen as boring, smug, self-interested, authoritarian, patriarchal, bureaucratic, and hypocritical. [175: 541]

Moreover, with minor exceptions, such as in Paris where brutal police action actually raised the sympathy of the local population for the students' demands, the protests never reached mass proportions.

Although the cultural and social significance of the protests of 1968 would be considerable, their immediate political consequences were limited. In France, they forced President de Gaulle to step down. De Gaulle finally departed in April 1969, after he had narrowly, and unexpectedly, lost a referendum on constitutional reform. But in almost all Western European democracies, the 1968 generation

48

would eventually bask in the warmth of the welfare state, which they themselves had initially critiqued and then opened up and expanded. Europe's national democracies proved robust and flexible enough to absorb the first serious post-war blows, which was the case even in those countries where the protest movement would take a violent and clearly anti-democratic course, as in Italy and Germany.

In both of the loser states of the Second World War, violent urban guerrilla movements appeared almost simultaneously. The Brigate Rosse (Red Brigades) in Italy and the Rote Armee Fraktion (RAF) or Red Army Faction in the Federal Republic of Germany were two major examples of the 1968 protest movements becoming violent, expressively going beyond the parameters of the post-war democratic order. During the early 1970s, the RAF committed a series of terrorist assaults on American military bases in Germany and on German government agencies, businesses and influential individuals. The urban guerrilla attacks of the RAF put the government in Bonn under great pressure. The German authorities proclaimed so-called *Berufsverbote*, which excluded individuals who had engaged in 'unconstitutional activities' from a range of public offices. But as ugly, threatening and polarized the political atmosphere was in Germany during this decade, with hindsight neither the RAF nor any other manifestation of violent opposition in Germany succeeded in fundamentally jeopardizing or undermining the democratic order.

Where did this opposition against the democratic state in Germany come from? The answer is often found in the remarkably quiet and unruffled transition from the widely supported and murderous Nazi dictatorship to the prosperous, law-abiding, *petit bourgeois* Federal Republic. Why had the war generation never been held accountable for their crimes or their indifference, young people asked? According to many left-wing students, there was no substantial difference between 'fascist' Germany before and pseudo-democratic Germany after the war; they considered the latter one as a client state of the imperialist United States. The students shared an obvious victim complex, Judt argues, one that was at least as strong as the guilt complex that they tried to force on their parents. He points to the national dimension of the political beliefs that inspired the RAF and its ancillary offshoots:

> The distinctly nationalist tinge to German extreme-Left terrorism
> – its targeting of American occupiers, multinational corporations

and the 'internationalist' capitalist order – rang a chord, as did the terrorists' claim that it was Germans who were the victims of the manipulations and interests of others. [87: 471]

The brief and dramatic history of the Red Army Faction was exceptional, and comparable only with the activities of the Red Brigades in Italy. In March 1978, left-wing extremists kidnapped the former Italian Prime Minister Aldo Moro (1963–8, 1974–6). After hiding him for 55 days, they killed the Christian Democratic politician and left his body in the trunk of a Renault 4, parked in the centre of Rome.

The acts of terrorism of the Rote Armee Fraktion, inspired by the alleged unwillingness of the German nation to account for its Nazi past and its submission to the European Community and the transatlantic alliance, triggered an ever more pronounced debate among conservative and progressive German intellectuals on the country's recent history and its national and historical identity. Film-makers such as Hans-Jürgen Syberberg, Rainer Werner Fassbinder and Edgar Reitz, internationally renowned writers such as Heinrich Böll and scholars of diverse views as the conservative historian Ernst Nolte and the liberal philosopher Jürgen Habermas joined a discussion on Germany's national past and identity, which raised extraordinary strong political emotions, within and beyond Germany. No contribution to the discussion on Germany's national past drew as much attention as the article that Ernst Nolte published in the perfectly respectable daily *Frankfurter Allgemeine Zeitung* in June 1986. The title said it all: 'The Past That Will Not Pass: A Speech That Could Be Written But Not Delivered'. Nolte strongly criticized the dominant historical interpretation of national socialism, and he bemoaned the taboo on anything that even remotely resembled a more positive and self-confident sense of German national identity. Nolte's article started what would become known as the *Historikerstreit* (literally the 'struggle among historians'), easily the most notable debate among historians in Germany, and elsewhere in Europe, during the Cold War [8]. Nolte argued that the 12 years of national socialist rule had to be lifted from its historical isolation. The Third Reich, he asserted, could not be truly understood without taking into account its most important 'conditions of origin': the Bolshevik Revolution and Stalinist dictatorship in Russia. Nolte criticized the ongoing 'demonization' of the Third Reich and the political manipulation of its commemoration. The effect of the article was explosive. What Nolte understood as historicizing the Third Reich, to narrate it as history instead of absolute evil beyond explanation, most of his opponents took for an act of exoneration. Nolte's work would remain hugely controversial, but it also set a trend. His reputation as a scholar of fascism became permanently tarnished, but his reassessment of interwar German and European history as a 'European civil war' [128] generated a considerable response. And especially after the Cold War, the comparison between Nazism and communism would lose most of its political sensitivity. In a sense, Nolte paved the way for a new direction of historical research and a novel aspect of public remembrance in Germany, regarding the sufferings of the *German* population during the war, from the atrocities committed by invading Soviet troops and from the terror bombing campaigns by British and American air forces. In the terminology of the debate, the *Historikerstreit* would free a substantial part of Germany's intellectual community from its national guilt complex.

Alarmed by the growing national self-awareness of many of his compatriots, Jürgen Habermas elaborated a new concept of national identity, a new patriotism, which did not take the nation, and much less so the ethnically defined nation, but the country's democratic, pro-European orientation as it focal point. Habermas's *Verfassungspatriotismus* or 'constitutional patriotism' represented an über-civic understanding of the nation and national identity. Although it attracted sympathetic attention among Germany's left-wing politicians and intellectuals, it never struck a chord in society at large. It was too thin, too rational. 'Constitutional patriotism remains a thing of the mind, not the heart', another preeminent political philosopher of German descent, Ralf Dahrendorf, wrote in *The Times* of 9 November 1990. 'It does not satisfy the need of many to live by and pass on to future generations deep structures of life in society' (quoted in [130: 115]). In any event, the atmosphere in Germany had changed. Issues that were once preferably toned down, such as national identity, ethnicity, multiculturalism and German victimization, had lost their sensitivity. They were no longer taboo. From the 1990s, when immigration and multiculturalism became an issue of public debate in Germany, in a similar way to many of its neighbouring countries, a German *Leitkultur* or dominant culture was openly discussed as a prerequisite for integration in German society, in the nation's common interest.

Regionalism, immigration and national identity

A distinct manifestation of nationalism in post-war Europe is better known as regionalism. Regionalism comes in different shapes and forms. It closely resembles nationalism, especially when it comes at the sub-national level, when it concerns a form of identity which is historically rooted and influenced by real or perceived cultural distinctiveness. Examples are Basque regionalism, and forms of regionalism in Catalonia, Corsica, Northern Ireland, Scotland and Wales, Flanders, Transylvania in Romania, Western Ukraine, Kosovo before independence and Friesland in the Netherlands. This variant of regionalism is often linked to the presence of ethnic minorities with a pronounced sense of identity, concentrated in a specific territory. In many cases, these minorities are culturally distinct from the dominant population group, in religion, in language or in less discernible ways such as ethnic or historical identities.

In addition to this variant of regionalism, commonly linked with 'historical', territorially concentrated minorities (therefore territorial minorities), from the 1970s onwards Western European countries have also seen other, rapidly growing minorities within their borders, namely immigrants, including non-Europeans (immigrant minorities). Among these minority groups are émigrés from Pakistan and India in Britain; from northern and other parts of Africa in France, Belgium and the Netherlands; and from Turkey, especially in Germany. Starting from the 1990s, Eastern Europeans added to this immigration movement, initially mainly from the former Soviet Union, especially people of German 'origin', followed by refugees from the Balkans, mainly due to the civil war in Bosnia, and labour migrants from the new EU member states of Poland, Romania and Bulgaria. Many of these immigrant minorities were able to keep a strong connection with, and commitment to, their countries of origin, which perpetuated their cultural distinctiveness from the majority of the population. In this context, Benedict Anderson introduced the expression 'long-distance nationalism' [5: 59].

During the years immediately following the Second World War, borders in Europe were redrawn, people were expelled from their homes and minorities were shifted across borders on a massive scale. Public and political opinion remained largely indifferent. The territorial minority issue (or regionalism) stayed dormant in most European countries until the 1960s. The new sense of minority identity that took political shape during those years occurred throughout Europe but was most manifest in the Western part of the continent. The ambitions of national minorities came in different varieties. Initially, they mostly translated into a commitment to political and cultural autonomy. Apparently, minorities expected that their ambitions could be realized within the framework of the national state, and thus in combination with a national political identity. Most of the population groups mentioned above – the Scots, the Welsh, the Flemish and others – belonged to this category. In those instances, however, where cultural identity was linked to *political* regionalism, to a drive for full autonomy or to even independence (separatism), serious political problems could arise. These difficulties were often enhanced by the strategies by which minorities' organizations chose to realize their ambitions and by the counter-initiatives taken by the national authorities. Among the most persistent problems were the armed struggle of the Irish Republican Army against British rule in Northern Ireland from the late 1950s and the struggle for independence by the ETA in northern Spain, which began around the same time.

Political regionalism is triggered by the discrepancy felt by inhabitants of a specific region between their 'sense of community' and the 'political arrangement' they are part of [91: 14]. Apparently, few scholars expected this to occur in post-war Europe. The wave of assertiveness among minorities from the late 1960s took them by surprise. The virulence of 'ethno-nationalism' [156: 125], 'sub-state nationalism' [164: 102] or separatist nationalism was a complete puzzle for most researchers. Especially, regionalist ambitions by relatively well-off parts of the population in some of the most highly developed and democratic nation states of Europe seemed difficult to explain. In a similar way to nationalism, regionalism and separatism were also widely considered as typically archaic phenomena, as legacies from another time and place. The political and socioeconomic context of most of Western Europe, defined by liberal democracy, an expanding welfare system and an advanced form of integration, had generated such high levels of freedom and prosperity that territorial separatism seemed to have become obsolete. Why would one want to disengage from countries which apparently offered every opportunity to enjoy one's personal freedom and collective identity? The communist countries of Eastern Europe may have been a different story. The Soviet Union was generally considered as a worthy successor to Tsarist Russia, once generally characterized as a 'prison of nations'. Its multinational nature was frequently mentioned as the Achilles heel of the Soviet empire. Were it ever to fall apart, the minorities' issue would certainly be a crucial factor – an argument that ultimately needed serious qualification, as the next chapter will elaborate.

How can the revival of regionalism in Europe from the 1960s be explained? The failure to notice the persistence of regional identities has been attributed to the dominant modernization paradigm in social and political science since the 1950s, which tended to underrate the continued relevance of 'ethnicity' as a factor in political change, and especially in national identity and nation building. The political scientist Walker Connor was an exception. He continued to emphasize that ethnicity would not wane as modernization progressed. 'The opposite is the case', he argued. Ethnic nationalism was mostly identified with its overt, radical expressions, and not seen in terms of its deeper, more permanent quintessence, he argued. Scholars generally overestimated the material dimension and the structural determinants of political behaviour, such as class, to the detriment of its cultural, its ethnic aspects [31: 41–5]. But then how to explain the particular timing of the resurgence of regionalism in Western Europe? General explanations such as the theory of 'internal colonization', which stresses peripheral minorities' subordination and discrimination by the dominant population group [67], fail to cut the mustard. They can neither explain why minorities who may enjoy higher standards of living than the majority population would rise against the national state, nor do they answer the question of when predominantly cultural regionalism develops into specific political ambitions. Connor concluded that there is no correlation between degrees of separatist nationalism and economic conditions. More important in his view was the growing density of communication, which enabled an ever-deeper penetration of the dominant culture into society. This apparently triggered the awareness and appreciation of minority groups' own different and specific collective identity. Cultural rather than economic deprivation generated regionalism [31: 153, 38].

Connor is right to question the importance of economic deprivation as a variable of regionalism. This does not imply, however, that economic variables were irrelevant. Economic motives do appear to be an important ingredient of political separatism in Europe, but indeed for reasons of relative wealth more than poverty. In many cases, regionalist ambitions based on feelings of discrimination or disadvantage came from regions' more advanced rather than backward positions. Relatively highly developed, well-off and dynamic parts of the country opposed the redistribution of income in favour of poorer regions within the framework of the national state. Nationalist parties in Flanders showed evident aspects of this economically inspired regionalism. They no longer accepted the alleged subsidization of Wallonia by the central government in Brussels. The discovery of oil off the coast of Scotland increased popular support for the region's political autonomy or independence. The belief that regionally produced wealth was unfairly distributed by the central state at the expense of those who actually generated it offered a powerful incentive to nationalist or separatist action in Czechoslovakia (the Czech Republic), in Yugoslavia (Slovenia and Croatia), in the Soviet Union (among the Baltic populations) and among the Basques and Catalans in Spain. In northern Italy, the protagonists of Padania believed that the government in Rome dedicated too many resources from the industrious northern part of the country to its corrupt and indolent regions in the south. The Lega Nord party (Northern League, founded in 1991 in Bergamo) combines a superficial appeal to the historical links of the northern Italian city states and the Holy Roman Empire with a regional, prosperity-based selfishness and a clear sense of superiority with regard to the country's regions south of Rome. The Lega Nord challenges the narrative and the reality of the national unity of Italy, two points that were inevitably compromised by the party's participation in national government. The political ambitions of the Lega Nord could be defined as 'material interests ... transformed into (national, ag) values' [18: 186]. The party has always remained in a minority position though. Even in its own heartland, the popularity of the Lega Nord would never reach that of Berlusconi's Forward Italy movement, or Forza Italia. So the weight of the economic argument is of importance, although it differs per case, and it always needs the additional sense of cultural and regional identity to gain political relevance. And even then, it does not explain why feelings of cultural distinctiveness remained dormant for decades, to suddenly and often unexpectedly gain political urgency and momentum.

As to the timing of regionalism, it seems that a combination of domestic and international political change during the Cold War created the opportunity and the urgency of separatist nationalism. The previously signalled gradual loss of political and social consensus and conformism in Western Europe played a role. The era of post-war reconstruction was reaching its end, and so were the logic of traditional authority relationships and the evident cultural hegemony of the nation state. In addition, the growing influx of mostly non-European immigrants strengthened the awareness and the recognition of multiculturalism within the nation state. International political developments have played a role too. The decolonization process and the doctrine of national self-determination offered inspiration, while the global conflict between East and West allowed for political and material support by some communist regimes. Finally, the process of European integration may have been of importance. Not only did European integration temper the perceived repressive political and legal 'monopoly' of the national state, but it also stimulated regional cultural and administrative diversity and development. For this purpose, a Regional Development Fund was set up in Brussels in 1975. In 1992, the member states of the Council of Europe adopted the European Charter for Regional or Minority Languages. Not only did the European Union acknowledge or promote regional identities, but it also facilitated separatist ambitions by 'softening' its potentially negative consequences. The official policy of the Scottish National Party developed from 'Independence – Nothing Less' during the 1970s to 'Independence in Europe' from the 1990s [164: 112]. The party's ambitions had not changed, but it sounded more moderate and for some Scottish voters probably considerably more acceptable.

The diversity of regionalist or separatist sentiments in Western Europe defies generalization on history, content and consequences. Scottish nationalism has a particularly strong ground in distinct organizations, such as the Church of Scotland and a separate legal and educational system. The Welsh lack these institutions but do enjoy a strong sense of cultural affinity. Relative poverty or relative wealth can both be incentives for separatism, either to secure or prevent a more 'equal' sharing of the national pie. Post-war separatist nationalism tended to be stronger among the more advanced and rapidly developing nations of Europe than among the poorer and more backward ones. While separatist nationalism is almost always based on a distinct, commonly shared language, religion or history, the political form it takes varies greatly and generally depends on the wider political context, which separatists cannot always influence. Administrative reforms which significantly meet the political demands and the aspirations of regional minorities had different consequences in different situations. Reforms could mitigate the concerns and ambitions of separatist movements and help to eventually solve the issue, as the early example of South Tyrol showed. They could diffuse the problem through the isolation of the radical, sometimes violent minority among the nationalists. But democratic reforms could also strengthen the case for separatist nationalism by enabling its political representatives to use legitimately democratic means to further their claims, as is illustrated again by the Scottish case. More than two decades into the post–Cold War era, the Scots almost gained independence, and through perfectly democratic means. Only a small majority of 55.3 per cent of voters prevented the region's full independence from the United Kingdom in a referendum in September 2014.

Over the course of the last two decades, the political centre of gravity of the minorities' issue in Western Europe shifted from the territorially based minorities to the new immigrant minorities, mostly from outside of Europe. Migration became a crucially important and highly controversial issue in Europe. It has its origins in the decolonization process and in the long years of almost uninterrupted economic growth during the Cold War decades. In the first years after the war, migration concerned mainly emigration from Europe, to the New World, to the United States, Canada and Australia. From the 1960s, however, the focus of migration changed to immigration, initially within Europe, from countries in the south to the north, and later into Europe, from parts of Africa and Asia.

Despite a considerable influx of newcomers over many years, no European country ever considered itself as a country of immigration. What gradually changed into multinational states have for a long time remained 'nation' states in perception. Germany is one of the European countries with the longest history of immigration and the largest amount of immigrants. German citizenship is based on the *jus sanguinis* principle. Nationality is defined by descent or ethnicity. This principle has distinct consequences. Immigrant families from Turkey could live in Germany for decades without being formally eligible for citizenship, whereas ethnic Germans from Eastern Europe, whose families may have left the German lands centuries ago and who often did not speak a word of German, had an automatic right of citizenship under the German constitution. Directly opposite to the 'ethnic' model of citizenship, primarily grounded in descent, is the French version, based on the *jus soli* principle: nationality is essentially defined by where a person is born. It affirms the inclusive and assimilationist nature of France's legal conception of nationhood and citizenship. It is the legal expression of the cultural and political idea that the 'nation' is one and indivisible – *la république une et indivisible* [20].

These divergent concepts of citizenship reflected different perceptions of the nation, or 'prevailing idioms of nationhood' [19: 162], and different national 'trajectories'. 'France was a "state" long before it was a "nation" ' [84: 101]. The French state knows a long centralizing and assimilationist tradition and became the principal agent and the prime object of national identification. French nationalism begins with the state. National identity developed within the political and territorial confines of the existing state. Germany on the other hand lacked the tradition of a strong and centralizing state. There was no German state until 1871. German identity was shaped by the nation, not by the state. The German lands were a nation, a *Volk*, in search of a state.

There were two major sources of immigration into post-war Western Europe: economic growth and decolonization. After the war, the most industrialized countries of Europe would develop an increasing appetite for additional labour. This need was initially satisfied within individual countries, by a trek among citizens from the countryside to the cities. Industrialization stimulated urbanization. Later, migration would grow between European countries, especially from the southern to the north-western parts of the continent. Italian, Spanish and Portuguese men and women started small businesses or went to work in the households, the coal mines and the factories of France, the Low Countries, and the German Ruhr in particular. In the early 1960s, the first 'guest workers' from Turkey and Northern Africa came to Western Europe, often after careful selection by receiving countries. They were mostly young men, uneducated and coming from the countryside. They were welcomed under the presumed condition that their stay would be temporary.

In addition to this labour-related immigration, there was also a considerable increase of immigrants from the former colonies. Post-colonial immigration came in different waves. First, the European settlers and their closest indigenous collaborators arrived in the metropolis. Later, non-European residents of the former colonial possessions followed suit. The Netherlands received tens of thousands of overseas citizens from its former colonies, initially from the East Indies and later also from the Antilles and Surinam. The United Kingdom received large numbers of immigrants from India, Pakistan and Bangladesh. Of the more than 1 million migrants who settled in Britain during the 1960s, the vast majority came from the British Commonwealth [175: 571–2]. France became the home of millions of people from North Africa, mostly French Algerians. Between 1955 and 1974, total immigration in France reached 4 million people, including a significant portion from other mostly Southern European countries. With important exceptions, such as the hostage crises by Moluccans in the Netherlands during the 1970s and the subversive activities by the *pieds-noirs*, the French in the overseas territory of Algeria, around the time of the Algerian War of Independence, immigration from former colonies rarely raised major political attention. This was even more the case with immigration from other European countries and from countries such as the United States, Australia and Canada.

Immigration did however significantly change the demographics of Europe. It transformed the continent from one of emigration to one of immigration. Between 1965 and 2000, the foreign-born population of Europe increased from 2.2 to 10.3 per cent. The impact was particularly strong in the larger cities. Immigration reached an all-time high between 1989 and 1993, immediately after the Cold War and during the violent conflicts in the former Soviet Union and Yugoslavia, hitting over 1 million people annually. It then levelled off to around 600,000 per year [27: 561–2].

The British government was among the first in Europe to attempt to control immigration. Already during the early 1960s, restrictions were placed on entry into the United Kingdom, especially among 'non-white immigrants'. 'The history of British regulation of immigration was one of ad hoc measures, strongly influenced by electoral considerations', by the 'expected reaction' of the British population, as the historian Malcolm Anderson [6: 57] writes. Elsewhere in Europe, most countries retained their relatively liberal immigration policies up until the 1980s or later, and rather few mainstream politicians showed a deeper interest in the societal consequences of immigration. This changed only gradually. For a long time, problems such as the concentration of poorer immigrants in certain urban districts and their continuing isolation from the rest of the population remained largely masked by the idea of multiculturalism. Multiculturalism supports the notion that ethnic or national minorities should achieve self-fulfilment as they aspire. The national state was not supposed to give special weight or relevance to a dominant culture or identity. Multiculturalism was as much built on the idea of cultural sovereignty and equality, as on a suspicion of state intervention into these matters [132].

The atmosphere, and with a considerable delay the political discussion, changed from the late 1980s. Not every Frenchman held the assimilationist French concept of the nation, and not every German continued to believe in the dominant multicultural German idea of the nation. The French elite's idiom of nationhood was probably more assimilationist and more statist than that of many French citizens [19: 235]. And there is reason to believe that the idea of multiculturalism persisted longer among the German political elite than among the general population. From the 1980s, both the French and German concepts of the nation came under increasing critique, and they were eventually adjusted. They carefully converged. Germany broadened its exclusionary model of nationhood and citizenship. But only in 2000 was legislation enacted that gave children of immigrants, who were legally resident in the country for at least eight years, the right to German citizenship. In 1993, France had already abolished the provision of automatically accorded citizenship to children of foreign parents born in France.

The gradual awareness of the challenges that the scale of immigration was causing would eventually instigate passionate political debate in most (West) European countries. Integration or assimilation of immigrants, never a true priority of any European government, became a hot issue. Immigration, especially of non-European ethnic groups, would become one of the most virulent 'national' political questions in post–Cold War Europe. Migration changed Europe. Where migrants settled in large numbers, they not only generated a greater awareness of other cultures among Europeans and initially a greater sense of tolerance for their differences [57: 560], but they also produced new ruptures, new lines of division, new complications. The political implications of large-scale immigration in Western European countries will be examined in the next chapter on Europe after the Cold War. But first another, much less discussed but typically Cold War, issue shall be discussed: the remarkable and uneasy alliance of communism and nationalism in Eastern Europe.

Nationalism and communism in Eastern Europe

From a strictly theoretical perspective, communism and nationalism are generally considered as opposites, especially from the perception of those who adhere to them. Most communists believed that irrational, unpredictable and anachronistic nationalism was fully incompatible with the rational, science-based and progressive world view of Marxism. Most nationalists followed the opposite logic. Socialists, communists and the like were considered as rootless materialists, who missed the essence of all things political: the nation.

Both in theory and in practice though, the relationship between nationalism and communism was much more ambiguous. As political ideas or doctrines, they overlap considerably. Nationalism and communism are both secular belief systems, with apparent analytical and prescriptive ambitions. They share a linear idea of history, an unequivocal belief in a better society and how to get there and a clear perception of who the enemies are. Nationalist and communist policies are equally deterministic, millenarian, confrontational and utopian.

The ambiguous relation between nationalism and communism can easily be recognized in the ideas of the intellectual founding fathers of socialism, Karl Marx and Friedrich Engels. Marx and Engels shared an instrumental and opportunistic view of nations and nationalism. Their distinction between reactionary (historically irrelevant) and progressive (historically relevant) nations was typical. Marx and Engels generally had little consideration for the separatist nationalism of small nations. This was deemed archaic and reactionary. It stood in the way of historical progress. While they saw nationalism essentially as a manifestation of false consciousness, they were prepared to support it whenever it contributed to the revolutionary struggle of the working class.

In the messy practice of nineteenth- and twentieth-century European politics, nationalist ideals and socialist and communist ideology proved far from incompatible. Nationalism served multiple purposes in the political struggles by communists and socialists. At critical moments, national and nationalist feelings proved significantly stronger than internationalist ideas, as was evident among many socialists at the outbreak of the Great War. Socialists often endorsed the imperialist and colonial ambitions of their conservative compatriots and frequently displayed an inflated sense of patriotism and national superiority. After the Second World War, socialists and communists were divided on the colonial issue, but they tended to support the struggle against imperialism and for national liberation, including the nationalist aspirations of post-colonial leaders. For their part, communists were more than eager to support the national interests of the Soviet Union, albeit from a quasi-internationalist position.

No other aspect of post-war European history revealed so well the ideological and practical closeness between communism and nationalism as did the communist states of Central and Eastern Europe. Nationalism and communism influenced each other deeply. Nationalist beliefs and ideas shaped communism. The communist regimes coloured nationalism. The linking aspect of the uneasy symbiosis between the two sets of ideas was political legitimacy. The communist parties in Eastern Europe attempted to legitimize their rule by explicitly invoking the interests of the nation and the nation state, through a special, sometimes cynical manipulation of national history, its heroes and symbols. Communist rulers constructed a new and strongly modified version of their nation's history and identity – not only to sustain their own rule, but also to disqualify and repress any real or perceived alternative. Nationalist arguments became an important tool in political struggles, within communist parties as well as between communist regimes and their opponents.

Most historians of communist Eastern Europe have emphasized the contrariety of communism and nationalism as political ideologies, while recognizing the significance of nationalism for most of the ruling parties in the communist part of Europe [22; 23; 96; 118; 186]. Communists were no exception to the many political entrepreneurs who employed nationalism for their own particular goals. Communist regimes appropriated some aspects of traditional nationalism, and ignored or rejected others. They presented a strongly deterministic vision of their nations' past, present and future, in which communist rule was of course considered as the high point and the end stage of national development. All the great leaders and all the great battles that could be pressed into the ideological straitjacket of the party state were embraced. In obvious contrast, all those aspects of the national past that could only be interpreted as either anti-communist or anti-Russian were conveniently ignored or shunned. Nationalism painted the 'official' history of the communist countries significantly.

Already in the early 1960s, Zbigniew Brzezinski, an influential American political scientist of Polish origin, referred to the obsession of the Eastern European communist leaders with their national histories, with their national symbols and heroes. He also observed how their concern for the national reputation of communism was not rarely at odds with their close alliance with the Soviet Union. Brzezinski [23: 52] did not explicitly mention nationalism but called it, more moderately, 'domesticism':

> a certain implicit perspective which is inevitably acquired by even the most loyal Soviet functionaries when they are assigned to specific tasks within the framework of more loosely defined ideological conceptions.

Other historians [118; 183] would considerably sharpen Brzezinski's earlier interpretation. Gradually, a consensus emerged on the extent to which communism was intertwined with nationalism. The Soviet Union proved no exception. The Soviet leaders not only developed a special amalgam of socialist ideology and Russian nationalist themes, but also allowed similar, though less pronounced, national variations of communism among the republics in the Soviet Union and among their allies in Eastern Europe. Essentially, all communism was national, Zwick writes [186: 89], as 'national communism' was the norm. Zwick's observation is correct, but it fails to mention the essence of the problem, namely how the national and international dimensions of communism are related to each other. Every communist regime had to take the wider international framework into account, that is the dominant communist ideology and type of international relations in Eastern Europe, as defined and demarcated by the Soviet Union. The crucial question is not whether, but how, to what extent and with what consequences national circumstances and nationalist ideas defined communism? This is an empirical issue, albeit with obvious normative connotations [139: 360]. During the Cold War in the West, specifically 'national' variants of communism were generally more favourably appreciated than regimes which faithfully towed the Soviet line. The extent to which a communist party availed itself of nationalistic propaganda or had emancipated itself from domination by Moscow proved no indication, however, of the degree of freedom it awarded to its own citizens. The differences between the communist regimes that were relatively free of Soviet interference were substantial. The Albanian communists broke with the Soviet Union from the early 1960s, and continued their fully orthodox and Stalinist party state until the very end, into the late 1980s. The Romanian regime had never cut its ties with the Soviet Union completely, but followed a relatively independent, albeit equally repressive, path from the early 1960s, especially under the leadership of Nicolae Ceauşescu (1965–89). The Yugoslav communist regime under Josip Broz Tito (1944–80) was forced to deal with a break with the Soviet Union in 1948. From there, it steered a non-aligned and relatively reformist course, but generally showed little compassion for its opponents inside and outside the Communist Party.

The national 'variations' of communism can only be understood against the background of the domination of the Soviet Union. Soviet hegemony and national communism remained locked in a particular dialectical relationship. One could not exist without the other. Stalin, who as a rule had little regard for the national interests of the subordinate communist regimes, was forced to accept a certain degree of national diversity among his allies, mostly as a strategic imperative. In general, the post-war domination of Eastern Europe by the Soviet Union was a phenomenal exercise in political *Gleichschaltung* or forced homogeneity. Eventually all communist countries under Soviet control followed the same trajectory of almost complete sovietization and full totalitarianism. With minor exceptions, national diversity was brutally subordinated to communist uniformity. Eastern Europe was recreated following the example of the Soviet Union, including the most glaring excesses of Stalinism: a rigid command economy, the full monopolization of power by the Communist Party, stifling censorship and a massive, sometimes absurd political terror, including show trials. The initial enthusiasm among many East Europeans for political and economic change, the anticipated response to the crisis of the 1930s and the suffering of the war years, evaporated in a short time. Many Eastern Europeans openly welcomed change, but there is little reason to believe that this enthusiasm was extended towards communist dictatorship.

There were two major exceptions to this general process of the sovietization of Eastern Europe: Finland and Austria. In a similar manner to Germany, Austria was divided between the four Allied powers. The Allies agreed to restore the sovereignty of Austria in 1955, on the specific condition, in response to demands from the Soviet Union, that the small Central European country declared itself forever neutral. On acquiring this agreement, France, Great Britain, the United States, and the Soviet Union withdrew their troops. Finland was another special case. Although the northern country fell under the Russian sphere of influence after the Second World War, it was never subject to full Soviet rule. Stalin accepted a democratic domestic order, as long as Finland's foreign and defence policies remained essentially loyal to the Soviet Union. Why the Soviet leader took such a benevolent stance *vis-à-vis* the Finns has never been determined with certainty. Whatever Stalin's motives may have been, 'Finlandization' became a household name in international politics. It stood for an independent, democratic course domestically in combination with a foreign policy that explicitly took into account the security interests of the Soviet Union. Over the course of the 1980s, when the prospect of far-reaching political reform in Eastern Europe became real, the option of Finlandization acquired renewed relevance. Inspired by political changes in the Soviet Union, non-communist oppositionists briefly debated the idea of domestic democratization under conditions of limited sovereignty. However, as we shall see, the geopolitical changes occurred so rapidly subsequently that the option of Finlandization was already obsolete before it could be seriously considered.

The *Pax Sovietica*, Russian rule over an important part of Central and Eastern Europe, was not an alliance in the conventional sense of the word. Relations between communist countries were not governed by the principles of national sovereignty and non-intervention but by a combination of highly unequal power relations (the military, economic and politic supremacy of the Soviet Union) in combination with ideologically inspired shared interests between a dominant and the subordinated states. The relationships between communist Russia and its allies were not based solely on coercion, however. The Warsaw Pact and the Council for Mutual Economic Assistance (COMECON), the East European counterparts of NATO and the European Community, were not merely instruments in the hands of Soviet leaders, as Cold War historiography generally portrayed them. Recent research reveals that Soviet allies secured and exercised considerable room to manoeuvre, especially within the Warsaw Pact from the mid-1960s [34]. This actually compelled the Soviet leadership to engage in continuous negotiations with its junior partners. Within the framework of the military alliance, all communist leaderships, not just the dissident ones, seemed to have had more political leeway than historians have long believed. Still, the Soviet Union was much more than just the dominant partner among equal allies. Ultimately, Moscow defined the practical as well as the ideological outer limits of communism in Eastern Europe – irrespective of the fact that it was not always willing or capable to enforce these. The Soviet Union's main leverage was the voluntary subordination by the national communist leaderships. Although this normative mechanism of control cannot be viewed in isolation from the material power instruments that the Soviet Union had, it was essentially based on the national communist leaderships' firm conviction that their political mission and survival ultimately depended on close relations with their powerful ally, the Soviet Union.

How did the communist regimes deal with the discordant pasts of their countries, and how did they reconcile the traditional national and nationalist controversies within and between their countries according to the parameters of the communist order? To begin with, the communist countries of Eastern Europe never really integrated with each other. Over the decades, the Soviet Union created an extensive network of mostly bilateral dependency relations, but the borders between the members of the Warsaw Pact remained practically as closed as those between the Eastern and Western part of Europe. The East European societies stayed largely separated from each other. There could not be any question of a free movement of people and ideas within the communist bloc. Behind the facade of communist brotherhood and proletarian internationalism, ongoing polemics were hidden. The communist leaders suppressed, concealed and denied national resentments and contradictions; they covered them with the mantle of ideological friendship, but they were unable and often unwilling to eliminate them. The metaphor of the *Pax Sovietica* serving as a thick layer of ice that froze the region's nationalism and national disputes for over 40 years is therefore only partly correct. The national issues were never really frozen. The communist regimes continued to struggle with them, and to opportunistically employ them. Nationalist arguments could be unapologetically manipulated. Yugoslavia and Albania bickered over the treatment of Albanians in Kosovo. Bulgaria and Yugoslavia fought a bitter conflict over the ethnic identity and the political loyalty of the Macedonians. Bulgaria saw Macedonians as Bulgarians, not as a separate nation; whereas in Yugoslavia Macedonians enjoyed the status of a separate nation, but were denied any form of statehood. Slovaks continued to harbour considerable distrust towards the Hungarians, both those at home and across the border in Hungary proper. The relations between Romania and Hungary were under heavy pressure for decades. Budapest raised severe criticism of the treatment of the Hungarian minority in Transylvania, while the Romanian leadership accused their Hungarian comrades of interference in its internal affairs. The Hungarian-Romanian conflict intensified as the two regimes continued to differentiate into a gradually more 'liberal' Hungarian and an ever more repressive Romanian variant of communism. Membership of the Warsaw Pact and COMECON averted a formal breach between the two countries, a situation not fundamentally different from the pacifying effect that NATO membership had on relations between Greece and Turkey. Nationalism and national contradictions were never placed in a freezer. They were an inherent aspect of communism. The communist rulers used them as an instrument for acquiring popular support and national legitimacy. It is only with hindsight that we know that these efforts proved largely futile.

Generally, there were two types of conflict between the communist states in Eastern Europe, and in both cases national and nationalist issues were involved. There were disagreements between the smaller states, of which some examples were given above, and there were conflicts between one or more smaller states on the one hand and the Soviet Union on the other. Especially in relations between the hegemonic Soviet power and its allies, the tension between the ideology of internationalism, which was largely defined and prescribed by the Soviet leadership, and the need to make concessions to the national interest, as perceived by its allies, played a prominent role. As a rule, these differences of interpretation remained hidden from the outside world, but on a few occasions, events developed into an open conflict.

The appearance of unity between the communist countries could only be upheld for a brief period of time. Already in 1948, a first break occurred in the communist camp, between the Soviet Union and Yugoslavia. The Yugoslav partisans had managed to liberate their country mainly by their own efforts, after the larger part of the German occupation forces had been moved to the eastern front, to fight against the advancing Red Army. The Yugoslav communists were loyal Stalinists. They voiced their annoyance about the arrogance and the meddling of Moscow, as well as about the unequal economic relations which the Soviet leadership tried to impose on them, but they never sought to break off relations with the Kremlin. It was Stalin who encouraged this rupture between the two communist countries. In March 1948, all Russian military advisers were suddenly recalled from Yugoslavia. Stalin strongly disapproved of what he considered as Tito's political radicalism. He criticized Tito's economic strategy, which would insufficiently serve the interests of Moscow, and he rejected Tito's foreign policy ambitions in the Balkans. But mostly, Stalin distrusted the Yugoslav leader for his autonomy, for his independence (see [30] for a documentary history of the Soviet-Yugoslav break).

In June 1948, Yugoslavia was expelled from the recently established Communist Information Bureau, or Cominform. The excommunication of Yugoslavia forced the leaders in Belgrade to formulate a new ideological legitimation of their rule. They rejected Stalinism, and returned to what they presented as 'real' Marxism-Leninism. They emphasized their own, national road to communism, of which the principle of workers' management was considered a vital component [30]. Although Tito would always hold to his national variant of communism, the feud with Moscow was settled after Stalin's death. During a visit of Soviet party leader Nikita Khrushchev to Belgrade in May 1955, both parties agreed to the principle that every state had the privilege to realize socialism at its own discretion and without outside interference. The Soviet Union accepted the national independence of Yugoslavia, both in theory and in practice.

But Yugoslavia was a special case. Tito was able to develop a truly national variant of communism, because he *was* independent. Different from practically every other country in Central and Eastern Europe, the Red Army had never occupied Yugoslavia. Stalin proved unable and his successors were not prepared to force Yugoslavia into line. The 1948 conflict was imposed on Tito, but without the Soviets being able to enforce their variant of communism. The Yugoslav leaders were therefore never compelled to engage in the delicate balancing act between their own national interests and those of the Soviet Union. Tito became the first communist leader who legitimized his rule partly on the basis of his differences with Moscow. In almost all other conflicts between the Soviet Union and its allies, the Eastern European leaders took a much more restrained position. They continued to stress the comradely nature of their relations with the Soviet Union, while carefully exploring ways to stretch the limits of the existing international order in their own national interest. Mostly this worked; sometimes it failed.

In February 1956, Khrushchev gave his 'Secret Speech' at the 20th Congress of the Communist Party of the Soviet Union. It was the unexpected beginning of a cautious de-Stalinization policy. Khrushchev's initiative aroused high expectations in a number of allied countries. In Poland, in October 1956, workers went on strike for a combination of social and political demands. The unrest reached such dimensions that the cornered Stalinist leadership was forced to reinstate former first secretary Władysław Gomułka, who had been under house arrest on charges of 'nationalist deviation' since 1948. The Soviet leaders were extremely displeased about this act of Polish independence or, as they called it, voluntarism. Not convinced of Gomułka's loyalty to Moscow, Khrushchev flew unannounced to Warsaw to personally berate the Polish communist leaders and force Poland back into line. Eventually, he accepted the reappointment of Gomułka, a decision he probably never regretted. Gomułka proved himself a loyal and orthodox communist.

He would remain in power until another workers' revolt, in the port city of Gdynia, which forced him to step down definitively in December 1970.

In the same October month of 1956, riots broke out in Hungary too. Here the ambitions were even more political, aimed at removing the Stalinist regime that had ruled the country since the Second World War. Within a few days, the revolt spread nationwide. Prime Minister Imre Nagy (1953–5, 1956) found himself at the helm of a rebellion which he had never really sought and which he could not possibly control. But Nagy played his involuntary revolutionary role with passion. He took two crucial, but fateful decisions: he abolished the power monopoly of the Communist Party and he announced the withdrawal of Hungary from the Warsaw Pact. By doing so, he took away the national and the internal fundamentals of Soviet dominance over Eastern Europe. The response from the Kremlin was swift and remorseless. On 4 November, Soviet troops pulled into Budapest and in just six days crushed the rebellion. Nagy had made a fatal mistake – literally, as it would transpire. Communist order in Hungary was restored, and Nagy would eventually be tried and executed on Soviet instructions. The prime minister's radical decisions had disrupted the fragile balance between the national interests of Hungary, as perceived by the rebellious communist leaders in Budapest, and the international interests of the Soviet Union, as understood by the rulers in the Kremlin. The Soviet Union's massive military capabilities ultimately prevailed.

Shortly after the crisis in Poland and the military intervention in Hungary, Soviet ideologists publicly addressed the tensions between the communist countries. They reworked the doctrine of socialist internationalism. The doctrine dictated that in the building of socialism, differences of opinion might occur between socialist states, to the extent that even conflicts might arise, but fundamental contradictions would be impossible. Other than in the capitalistic part of the world, disagreements or disputes between socialist states could only be non-antagonistic in form and transient in nature. Ultimately, national and international interests would always be harmoniously settled, and on the basis of free will [86: 128–9]. Reality would prove different again. In the early 1960s, another formal break in the socialist camp emerged, this time between the Soviet Union on the one side and China and Albania on the other. The communist regimes in Beijing and Tirana showed little sympathy for Khrushchev's political 'revisionism', and they considered the almost habitual interference of Moscow with the political developments in other communist countries, especially in their own countries, as totally unacceptable. Around the same time, the Romanian communist leaders rejected the supranational planning authority that Khrushchev had suggested for COMECON. Moscow advocated an international division of labour in which the Romanians would have to restrict themselves largely to the production of raw materials and agricultural products. Romania refused, and turned successfully against this violation of its sovereignty. The Romanian leaders would from then on combine an almost Stalinist orthodoxy in domestic politics with a substantial degree of independence in foreign relations. The communist regime in Romania greatly benefited from its autonomous stance. Party leader Ceauşescu became a celebrated international statesman. In August 1969, American President Richard Nixon (1969–74) visited Romania. It was the first visit ever by a US president to a communist country, except for the journey that Franklin Roosevelt (1933–45) took to Yalta in early 1945. Ceauşescu was warmly received in multiple Western countries. Romania was the first communist country that joined the World Trade Organization (at that time, in 1971, the General Agreement on Tariffs and Trade) and that was accepted into the World Bank and the International Monetary Fund. It was granted the most-favoured-nation status by the United States and by the European Community. Romania secured substantial loans, which Ceauşescu later regretted and would rush to repay at enormous costs for Romania's economy and its people's welfare. It took until well into the 1970s before Ceauşescu's independent international course would be overshadowed by his repressive, xenophobic and destructive politics at home.

In August 1968, differences of opinion ran high between a renewed, reform-minded leadership in Czechoslovakia and their Soviet, East German and Polish counterparts. The conflict accelerated to the point that the Soviet leadership, led by Leonid Brezhnev (1964–82) and under pressure from its conservative East European allies, decided to intervene militarily. On the night of 20–21 August, the Prague Spring, as the brief period of communist liberalization under Czechoslovakia's party leader Alexander Dubček (1968–9) came to be known, was violently crushed by the armies of the Warsaw Pact, minus Romania. Uninvited, 200,000 troops crossed the borders of communist Czechoslovakia, in what was the largest military operation in Europe since the Second World War. The invasion not only made clear again how fragile the balance between national and international interests in the Eastern bloc was, but also how insecure Soviet domination of Eastern Europe was at times of crisis. The fact that Soviet leaders intervened again in the internal affairs of an allied country, albeit under the pressure of some other allies, could be interpreted as a serious failure of its network of party, army and security links. In this sense, the gross violation of Czechoslovakia's territorial sovereignty was not so much a sign of strength but rather a revelation of the weakness of the *Pax Sovietica*, as was the refusal of the Romanian dictator and ally Nicolae Ceauşescu to consider participating in the invasion.

Immediately after the invasion of Czechoslovakia, the theory of international relations between the communist countries was explicated and re-emphasized again. In an article in the party organ *Pravda*, a certain S. Kovalov, a pen name for the highest leadership of the Soviet Union, laid out the notion of 'limited sovereignty', in the West referred to as the 'Brezhnev doctrine' [86: 153–8]. The core idea was simple and straightforward: the defence of socialism in one country was the concern of all countries. Once again, the Soviet leaders emphasized that the sovereignty of individual states was subordinated to the higher common interest of all states, as ultimately defined by the Soviet Union. The possibility of different paths towards socialism was recognized, but the idea of a national, that is an independent and autonomous, communism, whether in theory or in practice, was expressly rejected.

The invasion of Czechoslovakia and the overthrow of the Dubček leadership would be the final instance of Soviet troops intervening in the domestic affairs of an allied communist country in Europe. Hundreds of thousands of Soviet troops remained stationed in Eastern Europe, and they continued to be a power instrument of great significance, but they were never again mobilized to settle conflicts among communist allies. Actually, in a remarkable twist of history, 20 years after the intervention in Czechoslovakia, some communist allies would have greatly welcomed another mobilization of Soviet troops to defend the existing order. By that time, however, the political situation in the region had changed dramatically. In the late 1980s, Moscow was the major source of communist revisionism. Soviet party leader Mikhail Gorbachev had already indicated that he would not use Soviet troops to preserve the power of his conservative comrades in Russia's sphere of influence. In fact, he explicitly allowed his allies to go their own way, which under the given conditions could only mean that the orthodox communist order would either be reformed or, as it actually turned out, abolished.

The *annus mirabilis* 1989, when the communist regimes in all Eastern Europe an countries with the exception of the Soviet Union collapsed, was still unimaginably far away when the Polish People's Republic went through one of the most serious crises that a communist regime had ever experienced. The rise of the independent labour union Solidarność (Solidarity) in 1980, and the actual collapse of the communist party state that followed, created a power vacuum in the heart of Europe which would again be filled by military means, though this time by Polish troops, not Soviet ones. The Polish crisis had begun in the summer of 1980 when Polish workers had gone on strike once more. Their immediate demand was the revocation of the latest increase in food prices. The communist government applied its proven strategy of divide and rule, playing off one strike committee against another. This time, however, the strategy failed. After some hesitation, striking workers came together in the Lenin Shipyard in Gdańsk, on the Polish Baltic Sea coast, to form a national strike committee under the leadership of Lech Wałęsa. Wałęsa would later become the first chair of Solidarity. Aided by dissident intellectuals, some of whom had previously established the KOR (Komitet Obrony Robotników or Committee for the Protection of Workers), and on behalf of all their striking fellow workers, the Lenin Shipyard strike committee entered into negotiations with the communist government. The outcome of the talks, the Gdańsk Agreement of 31 August 1980, was astonishing and revolutionary. It would have far-reaching consequences for Poland and for the whole of the Soviet bloc. For the first time in the history of communist Eastern Europe, workers were allowed to organize their own independent trade union. They named it Solidarity. The Polish strikers had driven a huge nail into the coffin of the communist party state. In a few months' time, 10 million people, almost one out of every three Poles, joined the independent trade union. The mere existence of Solidarność was an enormous challenge to the ideological and organizational foundations of the Communist Party's leading role. The party had not only lost its *avant-garde*, the working class; it had lost its ability to rule at all. During the crisis, Poland transformed into a military dictatorship, which remained only communist in name. Solidarity was the beginning of the end of communism in Poland, if not in Eastern Europe.

It was with the utmost reluctance that the Soviet leadership accepted the unique concessions the communist authorities in Poland had made. The Soviet leadership interfered in the Polish crisis constantly, from the very beginning in the summer of 1980 – openly, covertly and behind the scenes. Moscow put heavy pressure on the regime of General Wojciech Jaruzelski, the Polish party, government and army leader, to restore order in the country and reinstate the power monopoly of the Communist Party. This was done through all available means: military manoeuvres in and around Poland, political consultations with allies and with alternative prominent communists in Poland and economic threats. Unlike in Hungary in 1956 and in Czechoslovakia in 1968, however, the Soviet Union did not intervene militarily. The differences between the Russian and the Polish leaders were tactical rather than principled in nature. The Kremlin compellingly insisted that the Polish communists themselves should solve their problems, and, ultimately, that is what happened. In the early winter morning of 13 December 1981, General Jaruzelski declared a 'State of War' (*stan wojenny*) in his country. He sent troops out into the streets of Warsaw and of other major cities and workers' strongholds in Poland to forcefully and definitely end the Solidarity experiment. The labour union was declared illegal. The power monopoly of the Communist Party was formally restored. In reality, the leadership of the armed forces remained firmly in control. For the duration of the State of War (1981–3), the Polish People's Republic was ruled by the Military Council of National Salvation.

General Jaruzelski legitimized the introduction of a State of War by explicitly referring to Poland's national rather than communist interests. When announcing his drastic measure, he appeared on Polish national television in full military regalia. He obviously wanted to convey the message that he had acted as Poland's supreme military commander rather than as its highest party leader. Jaruzelski asked for understanding from the Polish people. He presented the State of War as a choice for the greater good of the Polish nation and state, as a choice for the 'lesser evil'. Although he referred to the 'greater evil' only in vague terms, every Pole recognized it as the possibility of a Soviet intervention. Whether Jaruzelski's implicit reference to a Soviet military invasion was justified in reality is not the issue, although most probably it was not. The crucial matter is that he used the argument at all. Never before in Europe had a communist regime been saved by a military takeover, and never before had a loyal ally legitimized its national variant of communism with a reference to the threat of a Soviet invasion.

The significance of nationalism under communism clearly fits Breuilly's [17: 93] definition of nationalism as a form of politics. Also, in the communist countries of Eastern Europe, nationalism served the triple purpose that ideas or ideologies within political movements have in general: coordination, or the combination of diverging interests through the formulation of common ideas, mobilization of support and the legitimation of power. Was the manipulation of nationalism successful? It is difficult to establish whether and to what extent the communist regimes in Eastern Europe ever enjoyed real political legitimacy. Under communism, the mechanisms by which social support could be measured were non-existent, free elections and public opinion polls in particular. Some communist leaders may have occasionally had a firm measure of popular backing, perhaps even close to legitimate support, and nationalist beliefs probably played a role. This particularly applied to those communist regimes that did not directly depend on the support of the Soviet Union, such as the Yugoslav Communist Party, and to a certain extent to the Soviet regime itself. It may also have pertained to those communist leaders who at crucial moments resisted the interference of the Soviet Union and other allies, such as Nagy in Hungary, Gomułka in Poland, Dubček in Czechoslovakia, and maybe also to Ceaușescu in Romania during the initial phase of his increasingly repressive rule.

However, the popularity of a given party leader should not be mistaken for the legitimacy of communist rule. The fact that most of the regimes in the course of the post-war decades became less repressive and could count on at least the compliance of the vast majority of the population had relatively little to do with political legitimacy. This was in fact mainly the result of adaptation and resignation. The communist regimes seemed to have had an unspoken pact with their subjects, which secured political conformism in exchange for social mobility and rising living standards. During the course of the 1970s, however, this 'pact' came under increasing pressure. Most of the communist countries in Eastern Europe met with serious financial and economic problems. Economic growth decreased, turned into stagnation and in countries such as Poland and Romania into outright disaster. Scarcity returned as an ever more present aspect of everyday life in all countries. Societies became increasingly rigid and segmented. Social mobility became almost impossible. The communist order froze social relations and inequality. From the mid-1980s, real existing socialism began to look increasingly pale in comparison with the reinvigorating market economies in Western Europe. The gap between East and West was not bridged, as the communist regimes had promised, but actually widened. Crisis was in the air.

As Marxist-Leninist ideology lost general attraction and communist regimes encountered the limits of their socio-economic capabilities, nationalist arguments became an increasingly prominent aspect of the continuing quest for popular support. An optimistic, offensive and initially confident ideological legitimation, Marxism-Leninism gradually made way for a defensive and hesitant justification of communism by nationalist arguments. Acquiring political legitimacy on the basis of an appeal to the supreme relevance of nation and state proved a complicated task for communist regimes. As indicated, the communist movement could not boast of a rich history in Eastern Europe. In a predominantly agricultural region, with a working class of modest size, strong religious identities and a deep-seated mistrust of the revolutionary Soviet state, it was virtually impossible for communism to claim national allegiance. The communist regimes had few other options but to connect with non-revolutionary historical symbols and figures. Nationalist arguments were eccentrically selective and biased, and constantly changing, following the general political line [64; 118; 119; 139]. Party ideologues created their own mythology of the national past. They rewrote and manipulated the history of the nation on a constant basis. They appropriated its symbols and statesmen, they added their own heroes and holidays and they presented communist rule as the apogee of a progressive course of history. As the popular joke went, in communism nothing was as difficult to predict as the past.

Communist nationalism was an eclectic whole, carefully described in form and content by the powers that were. All communist regimes, orthodox or reformist, walked the same thin line, and variation was mostly due to specific national circumstances and to the particular nature of the communist regime. In the only ever officially religion-free society of Europe, the Stalinist outpost of Albania, party leader Enver Hoxha (1944–85) introduced 'Albanianism' as a secular religion, without much success. Paradoxically, when Hoxha died and his coffin was transported through the streets of Tirana, deeply distressed women crossed themselves openly. The communist leaders in East Berlin denied the existence of a common German people, and they represented the German Democratic Republic as a 'socialist nation' in a 'socialist German state'. These efforts also proved ephemeral, as events after the collapse of the Berlin Wall showed.

Although communist-style nationalism was pre-eminently secular, religion and the Church sometimes figured prominently in official national thinking. Traditionally, ethnic and socio-economic divisions often also had a religious dimension in Eastern Europe. Throughout the region, the dominant ethnic group often considered the Church as a pre-eminently *national* institution [140: 5]. During the communist era, there was a great deal of variety in relations between the Church and the state in the Eastern part of the continent, from pronounced enmity and ideological rivalry, to an uncomfortable *modus vivendi* or cooperation, but they always revolved around the (attempted) subordination of the Church to the state. The Protestant and Catholic Churches were generally in opposition to the communist regimes. They were tolerated in the GDR, Hungary, Yugoslavia and Slovakia, but they were suppressed in Romania, the Czech Republic, the Soviet Union and Albania. Only in Poland did the Catholic Church hold an exceptionally strong position. Such was the extent of its influence that the Catholic Church in Poland was able to force the communist regime to accept a political settlement. Due to the loss of eastern *Kresy*, the lands in the east which were mainly inhabited by Orthodox Ukrainian and Belarusian minorities, the almost complete destruction of the Jewish population and the expulsion of Germans after the Second World War, Poland had become practically ecumenically homogeneous. More than 90 per cent of the population was professed Catholic. And the conservative Catholic Church was considered by many in Poland as inextricably linked with the Polish nation and its dramatic history, as a beacon of national continuity. The communist regime, struggling to create at least a modicum of national legitimacy, could not afford to alienate the Catholic Church completely. The party's strategy towards the Church proved relatively effective. The Catholic Church in Poland identified with the larger part of the non-communist opposition, but always put its own interests first, including its *modus vivendi* with the communist party state. This position occasionally led to confusion and criticism on the part of the opposition, but the agreement with the communist regime lasted, and it enabled the Church to maintain, if not to strengthen, its social position and its political significance throughout the communist years.

The election of Karol Wojtyła, Archbishop of Kraków, as Pope John Paul II (whose pontificate lasted from 1978 to 2005) gave another boost to the status of the Church and the national self-awareness of the Poles. The Pope's first visit to his homeland, in June 1979, was an unrivalled manifestation of autonomy and independence – it was as if society had detached itself from the communist order and had become independent. In retrospect, the events seem to follow each other logically: from Wojtyła to Solidarność, to the State of War, and eventually and seemingly inevitably to the collapse of communism. At the time, however, each new phase in this chronology came as a surprise and ushered another period of tension and uncertainty. Communist rule in Poland effectively ended on 25 August 1989, when the government of Prime Minister Tadeusz Mazowiecki (1989–91) was sworn into office. The Catholic intellectual and oppositionist Mazowiecki led the country's (and region's) first post-war government that was not dominated by communists and their allies. It formally marked the end of communist rule in Poland. Other Eastern European countries would soon follow.

The Orthodox churches often took more conciliatory positions. They were mostly nationally based and were traditionally closer to the state, including under communist leadership. When communist rulers appealed to traditional, nationalist sentiments, they regularly found an ally in the Orthodox Church. After a period of repression and forced assimilation, the Orthodox churches in Romania, Bulgaria and the Soviet Union and, after the death of Tito (1980), also in Serbia mostly acted as advocates of the communist regimes, offering their secular rulers additional national credentials. They reconciled with their status of servitude, in exchange for a measure of internal autonomy and societal influence. In direct contrast to the Catholic and Protestant Churches, the Orthodox Church was an important instrument of official communist nationalism.

With the exception of the multinational Soviet Union, Yugoslavia and Czechoslovakia, the nationalisms of communist regimes almost always represented the nationalism of the dominant nation or ethnic group. National minorities were only partly or not at all integrated into the collective mythology of the nation and state. National and ethnic antipathies continued to simmer under the surface of socialist and internationalist conformism. The communist regimes tried in different ways to tackle the problem of ethnic diversity and national minorities [96]. Especially during the first years after the war, forced migration and border shifts were widely applied as appropriate methods of minority policies. Through the further homogenization of the population, the communist regimes sought to boost their legitimacy and to strengthen their power. The Soviet rulers used it as a means to cement their territorial sphere of influence.

The ethnic map of Eastern Europe has been considerably simplified over the course of the twentieth century. Ethnic minorities decreased from 25 per cent of the overall population during the 1930s to approximately 7 per cent in the 1970s. During and immediately after the Second World War, an estimated 23 million Eastern Europeans (four out of every ten inhabitants) were affected by voluntary and forced migration, genocide and border shifts [75: 35–107]. Although the Soviet Union generally opposed the territorial ambitions of its post-war allies, it itself annexed parts of Czechoslovakia (Carpathian Ukraine), Romania (Bessarabia and Northern Bukovina), Germany (East Prussia) and Poland's eastern provinces. The Soviet leaders and communist regimes in Eastern Europe supported the expulsion of the *Volksdeutsche* (to which the Western allies tacitly agreed) and the forced relocation of other population groups, including those of Hungarian Slovaks to Hungary and Slovakian Hungarians to Slovakia, of Ukrainians to the western part of Poland, of Bulgarian Turks to Turkey and of Romanians from Bessarabia and Wallachia to Transylvania. More than 11.5 million Germans, and those who were held to be German, were expelled from Eastern Europe. Many fled with the retreating German army; others were later forced to depart, mostly on short notice and often violently. This massive wave of migration, one of the largest in European history, effectively terminated a century-long history of German settlement in Eastern Europe. The destruction of Jews and the expulsion of Germans during and immediately after the Second

World War were two of the most dramatic chapters in the modern history of Eastern Europe. No other minorities had had a stronger impact on the administrative (legal) and the economic development of Eastern Europe than the German and Jewish populations. Although genocide, expulsion and 'voluntary' migration considerably changed the ethnic map of Eastern Europe, these forces had done little to diminish the sensitivity or the topicality of the minorities issue. While ethnic cleansing remained largely limited to the first years after the war, the idea of intervening in the structure of the population inspired by nationalist political purposes never disappeared from the repertoire of the communist regimes [168]. Even in the mid-1980s, communist rulers in Bulgaria drove a large number of Muslim Bulgarians ('Turks') out of the country. About 10 per cent of the Bulgarian population belonged to this minority, and an estimated 300,000 people fled to Turkey. Those who remained behind were subjected to a rigorous assimilation policy, including forced name change and restrictions on the use of the Turkish language. Ceauşescu repeatedly used the minorities' issue as a domestic and foreign policy instrument. The Jewish community in particular was an important pawn in his pursuit of international legitimacy and respect. As Ceauşescu once confided to the country's Chief Rabbi Moses Rosen: 'We have had fourteen ambassadors and 300 diplomats in the United States since 1945, but all of them together did not do as good a job for us as you did' [35: 205]. Nowhere, however, would the issue of minorities, especially with regard to the Jewish question, remain so conspicuously present as in Poland. In all communist countries, the Jewish question was a sensitive issue, but in Poland it continued to be a matter of significant national political weight [51]. In 1967, in an attempt to disarm the opposition inside and outside of the Polish United Workers' Party, party leader Gomułka invoked the spirit of an international Jewish conspiracy again. In the process, he portrayed Poland's Jews as unreliable citizens, as a 'fifth column'. Despite the fact that many Jews in Poland had to be forcefully reminded of their Jewish roots (such was their state of assimilation), the Gomułka leadership brandished them as traitors and forced them to leave the country. It would be the last government-sponsored anti-Semitic campaign in Europe, leaving aside the permanent anti-Zionist propaganda peddled by practically every communist regime till the end of the 1980s. Gomułka won himself another two years in power.

Repression, expulsion and forced assimilation of minorities were only part of the story. The history of ethnic minorities and of minority policies under communism is more complex and more ambiguous than these dramatic episodes suggest. On the whole, after 1948, national minorities were in a better situation than during most of the interwar period [96: 73]. In nearly every communist country, national minorities were eventually granted equal rights. For the first time in the history of most East European nations, individuals belonging to minority groups reached positions of political authority and power. Enforced adjustment and assimilation were initially paired with a remarkable degree of organizational and communal freedom, albeit within the limited parameters of the communist party state. With exceptions, minorities had their own cultural organizations. They often enjoyed (primary) education and press in their own languages. Obviously, political autonomy remained out of the question, but this applied to the whole of the population, minorities and majority alike. In the long run, communist regimes coupled political and ideological uniformity with a substantial degree of cultural diversity.

The renowned British historian Hugh Seton-Watson concluded in 1977 that only the Yugoslav communists had made real progress towards a solution to the continuing national problem in Eastern Europe [150]. By now we know that this assertion was premature, at best. The Balkan wars in the 1990s revealed that especially in Yugoslavia the demise of the multi-ethnic communist state was violent and bloody. In fact, as will be argued, the collapse of Yugoslavia and the conflicts that followed were causally linked to how the Yugoslav communists had shaped their multinational state, which in fact had followed closely the model of the Soviet Union.

The collapse of communism

Marxism-Leninism in Russia was the first and most important attempt to combine particular national conditions and interests with the universal claims and aspirations of Marxist ideology. After the Bolsheviks had secured power, following on their *coup d'état* in October 1917 and a vicious civil war from 1918 to 1921, they were forced to adapt to the reality of Russian society. In the wake of the Great War, the whole of the European continent was engulfed by revolutionary fervour, but the only successful socialist revolution took place in a country where it might have been least expected: Russia. Why in predominantly agrarian and relatively backward Russia? Not many historians go as far as Ernest Gellner, who suggests that Marxism was cut ('tailor-made') for the 'Russian soul' [50: 36], but the idea that many aspects of Russian culture and history made the country susceptible to communist rule is commonly shared. A long history of autocracy is often mentioned, as are the Orthodox religion, and a tradition of *étatisme*, collectivism as well as messianic and radical thought [108; 111; 134]. How can Bolshevik rule be assessed? Was it a logical continuation of Tsarist Russian history or rather a variant of Western Enlightenment thinking gone radically astray? In other words, was it tradition or was it ideology? The first argument says that communism in the Soviet Union should principally be understood as the outcome of the Bolsheviks' accommodation to the harsh realities of Russia, with the civil war, the country's international isolation (therefore 'socialism in one country') and its strongly agricultural character as important features [27; 38]. The second argument more convincingly suggests that many of the core institutions and practices in the Soviet Union can hardly be related to Russia's national past or traditions. This refers to the Communist Party's *avant-garde* role, to the planned economy, class struggle and proletarian internationalism. They were principally inspired by the dominant Marxist ideology [111]. The conclusion may be that Soviet rule was cloaked in Russian national reality but essentially shaped by Marxist ideology – an inference that is actually captured by the phrase Marxism-Leninism. Eventually, however, the two constituent aspects of Bolshevism would become fully intertwined. This also applies to how the Soviet leaders dealt with the 'national question'. Russian nationalism, proletarian internationalism, Soviet patriotism and other ideologically inspired notions, in combination with the actual position of ethnic groups, would become eclectically and inextricably linked in the nationalities' policies of the Communist Party.

In the Soviet Union as well in Eastern Europe, nationalism was also an important, though difficult-to-identify, factor in the downfall of communism during the crucial years 1989–91. Generally, the pursuit of democracy and of prosperity within independent and sovereign nation states were the dominant dual ambitions in most of the former communist countries. Alternative political beliefs initially remained under the surface. Democratic and national aspirations were for many Eastern Europeans naturally linked. Democracy could only be reached through national solidarity and full independence. Democracy needed nationalism. The communist order was generally considered as 'foreign', imposed by an outside power, be it Soviet, Russian or a combination. This proved to be one of the crucial paradoxes of communist rule in Eastern Europe, including the Baltic states of Estonia, Latvia and Lithuania. For practically every communist regime, the support of the Soviet Union represented both a lifeline and their 'weakest link'. The threat or reality of a Soviet invasion kept most communist regimes in the saddle for over 40 years, but the very same pact with Moscow made it practically impossible to gain a reasonable degree of political legitimacy. As hard as the communist leaders attempted to establish their national credentials, in the eyes of the majority of the populations, they remained puppets of the Kremlin.

The communist order in the Soviet Union and with variations in the other countries had been gradually eroded by a number of systemic contradictions, which would eventually make significant reform both inevitable and also practically impossible. Throughout their rule, the communist regimes had generally opted for short-term political stability at the expense of necessary longer-term economic change and modernization. The revolution in information and communication that was to transform Western society from the 1980s almost completely bypassed the communist countries. The major reason was political. The novel information and communication technologies could not possibly be reconciled with the rigid parameters of the communist political order. They would inevitably undermine the monopoly on truth and power which the communist regime had reserved from themselves. As a consequence, the economic and technological gap between East and West grew rapidly. The communist regimes were further weakened by the deepening contrast between a progressively more modern and pluralistic society and an inflexible political regime, which remained totalitarian in its monopolization of power. Paradoxically, the soft totalitarianism of the 1970s and 1980s, or 'totalitarianism with its teeth knocked out' as the Polish dissident and journalist Adam Michnik once phrased it (quoted in [99: 31]), seemed even more unbearable than its earlier more repressive variant. The communist regimes continued to deeply and oppressively meddle into the personal lives of their subjects, but refused to give them any meaningful role in how the country was run. Until the very end, communism remained a 'conspiracy in power'.

In assessing the significance of nationalism as a variable of communist collapse, a distinction should be made between the nation states in Central and Eastern Europe, largely ethnically homogeneous, and the three multinational states, Yugoslavia, the Soviet Union and Czechoslovakia. These multinational states collapsed and dissolved with the demise of the communist order. Economic egoism on the part of the Czech government, which sought to develop relations with the European Union without the ballast of the poorer Slovak part of the country, and the rejection of radical economic reform on the Slovak side, where the elite was narrowly linked with the heavy industry sector, determined the fate of Czechoslovakia. The 'velvet divorce' of Czechs and Slovaks in January 1993 was an act of superior political manipulation. It was the result of elite bargaining, which was never subjected to any form of popular vote. In contrast to Czechoslovakia, radical and popular political nationalism played a crucial role in the violent disintegration of Yugoslavia. Without downplaying the lack of political identification with the national state ('Yugoslavism') and the continuity of historical ethnic and national resentments in communist Yugoslavia, relations among the South Slavs were particularly poisoned by the unscrupulous political engineering and manipulation of its post-communist elites. After the death of Tito in 1980, particularistic nationalism became the prime tool with which political support was mobilized in Serbia and eventually in all constituent parts or republics of the country. The nationalist engineering by the country's political elites further challenged Yugoslavia's fragile inter-ethnic relations, fed by national resentments that had never been far from the surface and under heavy strain from the country's mounting economic problems. As will be argued in the next chapter, these elites consciously pushed the country into the direction of civil war.

The states of Czechoslovakia and Yugoslavia did not have a historical precedent. There had never been a common state of Czechs and Slovaks or of South Slavs. Czechoslovakia and Yugoslavia would not have been established without the efforts to redraw the map of East-Central Europe along national lines by US President Woodrow Wilson (1913–21) and his allies during the peace negotiations in Paris (1919). The formation of Czechoslovakia and Yugoslavia (or until 1929 the Kingdom of Serbs, Croats and Slovenes) was made possible by the victors of the First World War, who built on the nationalist aspirations of Czech and some Slovak and South Slav (especially Croatian) political figures. While political mobilization of nationalist sentiments was at the heart of the rise and the fall of two of Europe's major multinational states, generally nationalism *per se* neither creates nor destroys states. It is the propitious combination of nationalism and other political motives, ambitions and circumstances that gives nationalism its tremendous power – either creative or destructive in nature. This is how these multinational states were established, and this is why they collapsed again before the twentieth century came to an end.

Nationalism played an equally ambiguous role in the disintegration of the Soviet Union. Nationalist ideas became increasingly vocal and nationalist organizations progressively conspicuous during the last years of the Soviet Union. Nationalism was a major political force in some Soviet republics, especially in Estonia, Latvia and Lithuania, in the South Caucasus and to a certain extent in Ukraine, but it was practically negligible in others, such as in Belarus and in the republics of Central Asia. The struggle for independence was strongest in the Baltic states. The memory of a recent, brief history of independence during the interwar years, cruelly interrupted by Stalin's aggression, in conjunction with a still vibrant national identity and a comparatively high standard of living, provided the building blocks of strong nationalist political activities in the Baltics from the mid-1980s. In all three Baltic republics, communist parties fell apart and pro-independence movements were established. Largely free elections brought the opposition to power. In comparison with most other Soviet republics, popular participation and mass nationalist activity were particularly prominent. On 23 August 1989, about 1.8 million people, a quarter of the population of Estonia, Latvia and Lithuania, formed a human chain of more than 600 kilometres from Vilnius through Riga to Tallinn. They commemorated the 50th anniversary of the Molotov-Ribbentrop Pact, the deal between Hitler and Stalin whose secret annexe contained details of the division of East-Central Europe into a Russian and a German sphere of interest. The pact terminated the 20 years of independence enjoyed by interwar Estonia, Latvia and Lithuania. On 4 May 1990, the Supreme Soviet of Latvia voted in favour of full independence. Before, in March 1990, the Lithuanian parliament had taken a similar decision, by 124 votes for independence and zero against. Tallinn restored the pre-war Republic of Estonia on 8 May 1990. A violent crackdown by Soviet security forces in Vilnius and Riga in January 1991 – it still remains unclear on whose authority – could not anymore turn the tide. Boris Yeltsin, the democratically elected president of the Russian Federation, ignored Soviet President Gorbachev and agreed on the mutual recognition of sovereignty with the three Baltic republics.

It would still be a simplification to argue that the Soviet Union collapsed under the pressure of rising nationalist opposition against centralized communist or Russian rule. As previously argued, the political strength of nationalist movements, of nationalism, is hardly ever a sufficient condition for state disintegration or formation. The multinational Soviet Union was no exception to this rule. Neither could it be asserted that rising nationalism in Russia was simply a 'response' to the evident breakdown of state power as Breuilly [17: 350]) argues. Chronologically, however, the latter argument carries more weight than the former. The weakening of the communist party state, which resulted from Gorbachev's economic and political reforms, preceded, inspired and allowed for nationalist opposition, and not the other way around.

The demise of the Soviet Union was a unique historical event. For the first time in the history of Europe, an empire perished in peacetime, and primarily for internal political reasons. The ultimate disintegration of the Soviet Union developed in a complex process of intra-elite conflict, growing nationalist assertiveness in the periphery and in the centre, increasing political-administrative chaos and socio-economic crisis, and ultimately a massive lack of legitimacy among the general population and a substantial part of the elite. The struggle for sovereignty and independence in various Soviet republics, including in Russia, was evidently important. In particular, the declaration of independence by the Ukrainian parliament in August 1991, overwhelmingly supported by a nationwide referendum held a few weeks later, came as a highly unpleasant surprise to both Yeltsin and Gorbachev. It not only destroyed Gorbachev's ambition to keep a reformed Soviet Union together, but it also frustrated Yeltsin's attempts to build a new, post-Soviet union under Russian tutelage [136]. However, even the declaration of independence by Ukraine paled in comparison with the proclamation of sovereignty by Russia itself, on 12 June 1990, by the

First Congress of People's Deputies of the Russian Soviet Federative Socialist Republic. Russia did not exit the Soviet Union, but it kept the option open. Yeltsin and his political sympathizers used the autonomy of the Russian Federation as a tool to break the power of the old Soviet elite. As the Russian journalist Sergey Parkhomenko put it: 'when Russia's democratic forces proved unable to liberate the country from Gorbachev, they liberated Gorbachev from his country' (quoted in [141: 26]). A Soviet Union without Russia would be an empty shell, a political vacuum. Yeltsin's declaration of sovereignty together with the essentially non-violent strategy of movements for national independence in the other Soviet republics would eventually result in a historically unprecedented, little-anticipated, mostly peaceful disintegration of the superpower and the multinational empire that was the Soviet Union.

The demise of the Soviet Union occurred in a reverse process of decolonization. It was not so much the colonies that freed themselves from the colonizing power; it was the colonizer, in an act of supreme political manipulation, that broke away from the colonies. For a large part of the ethnically Russian population, the collapse of the Soviet Union came as a moment of shock. Russia had never been a colonial power like England, France or the Netherlands. The colonies of Russia were not overseas; they were within the physical and political borders of the state. Russia was a nation state and a colonial empire combined. 'The history of Russia', wrote its most prominent historian Vasily Kliuchevskii, 'is the history of a country that colonized itself' (quoted in [134]). Geographically, but also politically and in terms of identity, state, nation and empire had always been intimately linked in Russia. In this respect, the rapid and unanticipated disintegration of the Soviet Union was a considerably more traumatic event for the Russians than the disintegration of the British, French and Dutch overseas colonial empires ever was for the citizens of these West European powers.

However, in the years preceding the break-up of the Soviet Union, the Russians too seemed to have developed a new national awareness. An important aspect of their reclaimed national consciousness was the growing belief that the Russians had suffered as much from communism as the non-Russian peoples had, especially in terms of their 'national' identity. From 1917, Russian and Soviet identities had greatly overlapped both ideationally and institutionally. Given

the history of the empire, which expanded from a medieval princi-
pality in the heart of European Russia, and the political and, gradually decreasing, numerical dominance of the Russian population,
the Soviet Union was commonly identified as a *Russian* empire.
To a large extent, Russia *was* the Soviet Union, and vice versa. The
Russian Federation did not have its own communist party, Academy
of Sciences or state security – these institutions were all shared with
those of the USSR. From the Soviet perspective, therefore, Russian
nationalism was a particularly subversive issue. Assertive Russian
nationalism could easily destroy the politically defined, multinational identity of the Soviet Union. Still, a Russian national identity, even a Russian nationalism, never completely disappeared, and
they were even officially employed during the empire's moment of
greatest agony. Stalin conspicuously invoked the power of Russian
nationalism during the Great Patriotic War against Nazi Germany,
from 1941 to 1945. The greatness of the Soviet Union was the greatness of Russia and the Russians, and in their wake that of the other
republics and peoples. But Russia itself was a multinational entity
too. Hence, a distinction was often applied between the ethnic
and the civic understanding of being Russian. *Russkie* and *Rossiiskie*
referred to Russians as an ethnic group and Russians as the citizens of the Russian Federation. The growing national awareness
of many Russians particularly pertained to the Russkie, to the ethnic Russians, rather than to the ethnically non-Russian citizens of
Russia.

A more informal and unofficial 'reinvention' of Russian national
identity during the Soviet Union dated back to the 1970s, well
before the heady days of glasnost and perestroika. It was the combined result of a growing uneasiness among Russian intellectuals
over the demise of traditional Russian (material) culture and identity, including its environmental heritage, and the desire of the conservative leadership of the Communist Party to more firmly establish
its national credentials among the Russian population [22: 3]. The
attempt to catch up with the country's national past and traditions
was not fundamentally different from that of other communist
countries. Communism and nationalism may have actually been a
more effective political amalgam in the Soviet Union than in most
of the Central and Eastern European countries. In a large part of
the Soviet empire, and to some extent also in Yugoslavia, communism could be seen as a 'national' political order, and not as one

imposed by a foreign power, as it was felt in most other communist countries. Russian nationalism during late communist times was primarily conservative in nature. Already from the 1970s Russian authors, 'village writers' or *derevenshchiki*, voiced criticism of the dramatic impact of Soviet industrialization polices, particularly on the traditional life and culture of the Russian peasantry. Just like other publicists, village writers were subjected to the vagaries of state censorship, but, in practice, they enjoyed relative freedom of expression. Most of them were permitted to write for state publishers and official journals. Until the 1980s, they were among the most popular authors in Russia within the general population and a crucial part of the political leadership. Only after the death of Leonid Brezhnev and his chief ideologist Mikhail Suslov in 1982 did the village writers fall out of official favour. Gorbachev reportedly did not think much of their conservative social criticism. In fact, he viewed with anxiety how the type of Russian nationalism that the village writers represented gained increasing support among his conservative opponents within the Communist Party [22].

The village writers stimulated a strong interest in the rediscovery and preservation of Russia's past, in combination with a deep concern for the environment. They paved the way for a series of independent grass-roots organizations that were established during the early years of Gorbachev's rule. Among these non-official groups or *neformalnye*, a variety of nationalist organizations sprang up in all Soviet republics, including Russia. Pamyat (Memory) was one of the more popular and well-known nationalist groups. It set itself the task of defending Russia's endangered traditional values, restoring the nucleus of its popular culture, the village, and preserving its natural and historic monuments. Founded in 1987, Pamyat soon engaged in an unremitting struggle against the perceived demonic forces responsible for Russia's misfortune: from alcoholism and bureaucracy to Freemasons, Zionists and Jews [22: 204–5]. Although Pamyat would never become a mass movement, its eclectic nationalist platform attracted sympathizers from across the political spectrum. Radical Russian nationalism was manifest within the Communist Party as well as within its political alternatives from the late 1980s, most famously in the Liberal Democratic Party of Vladimir Zhirinovsky. Zhirinovsky's was a salon opposition party, persistently dogged by rumours that it was actually created by the KGB (Komitet Gosudarstvennoy Bezopasnosti or Committee for State Security) with the aim of becoming a controlled alternative to the Communist Party. Meanwhile, in 1990, Russian communists who were unhappy with the reformist course of the Gorbachev leadership established their 'own' Communist Party of the Russian Federation. Finally, Russia had its own Communist Party. The party strongly criticized the ideas and policies of Gorbachev as well as of Yeltsin and his democratic opposition. The Russian Communist Party was banned after the failed coup of August 1991, but it returned again after a legal ruling in February 1993. The Russian Communist Party would eventually develop into the country's major opposition party, albeit of a 'systemic' nature. Systemic is jargon for that part of the political opposition which remained loyal towards Russia's post-communist leaders, and which continued to operate within the limited parameters of Russia's increasingly authoritarian political order.

The Soviet Union, Yugoslavia and Czechoslovakia fell apart along 'national' and largely ethnic lines. The communist leaders had always been aware of the power of nationalism, of its supportive and its destructive potential. Their political strategies, however, remained ambivalent and proved ultimately counterproductive. Unlike in pre-war Yugoslavia or in Tsarist Russia, in the communist successor states, administrative and ethnic boundaries were largely congruent. The vast majority of Ukrainians lived within the borders of their 'own', quasi-autonomous Ukrainian republic, and so did the Soviet Union's other major 'nationalities'. Bilingualism was officially promoted in the Soviet Union, that is Russian and the native language. Russian may have been the indispensable *lingua franca*, but the local language played a crucial role in upbringing, early education and therefore in cultural awareness too. This combination of administrative borders and cultural policies helped to perpetuate the (national) identities of many minorities. Constitutional federalism may have been fiction in the Soviet Union, but the idea was not without important practical implications. The Soviet leaders continued or created, especially in Central Asia, the administrative-territorial units to which formal political autonomy was denied but which possessed many of the institutional and symbolic attributes of sovereign states, including their own political institutions and cultural and administrative elites [163]. The political and administrative 'backbone' of the Soviet system, the Communist Party of the Soviet Union, was indeed a highly centralized institution, but its leadership allowed for considerable republican autonomy, as long as the supremacy of the all-union Communist Party was not challenged. Ukrainian communists had always been prominently present in the top echelons of the CPSU, partly to cement the Russo-Ukrainian core of the empire. Three of the Soviet Union's post-Stalinist leaders were of (partly) Ukrainian descent: Nikita Khrushchev, Leonid Brezhnev and Mikhail Gorbachev. The Kremlin was traditionally willing to accept the strongly autonomous position and the deep corruption of the Central Asian communist leaderships, as long as they remained loyal to the Soviet party state. The Soviet Union was neither just the federation that it was in name, nor the strongly centralized state that it seemed in practice. It combined both features, in a complex, ambiguous and largely informal manner. The Soviet regime repressed nationalism, but it institutionalized a strong sense of nationhood and nationality [20: 17]. Efforts to create a radically new, a socialist 'national' identity through Soviet patriotism or 'Yugoslavism' proved not totally futile, but they would ultimately fail against the persistence of traditional sub-state national identities.

The concurrence of ethnic and administrative boundaries greatly contributed to the continuity of nationalism and eventually to the demise of the communist multinational states. However, it also provided a reasonable degree of consensus on the borders between the peoples and the republics aspiring for independence, at least within the Soviet Union. When Gorbachev opened up the political arena, oppositional parties and individuals easily mobilized support also on an ethnic ticket. When this developed into a struggle for independence, the administrative division of the Soviet Union, in combination with a considerable continuity of cultural and linguistic autonomy, had secured consent on where the borders between the newly independent states ran. In other words, the congruence between administrative and 'national' borders greatly contributed to the largely peaceful disintegration of the Soviet empire. This was no mean feat for a country that was stacked with conventional and mass destruction weaponry. It was a tremendously important aspect of the Soviet demise. A Yugoslav scenario of rampant nationalist conflict and civil war would have been a complete disaster for the peoples of the former Soviet empire, and for many beyond the Soviet Union.

3 Europe after the Cold War

The end of the Cold War had brought momentous change to the whole of Europe. Historians' interest has understandably focused on the Eastern part of the continent, where the collapse of communist rule and the disintegration of multinational states redrew the map of Europe and transformed the lives of its citizens. But Western Europe changed too. Western Europe had also been a product of the Cold War. Initially, the changes in the former communist and in the western part of Europe were very different, shaped by their diverging Cold War realities. Eventually, however, as the countries in Central and Eastern Europe left their communist pasts behind and entered the wider European realm, former East and West in Europe began to face similar challenges. The relevance of nationalism in these changes concentrates on three issues: state disintegration and formation in Central and Eastern Europe; the deepening and widening of European integration and the political responses it triggered; and, finally, the further increase of immigration and the hardening of the debate on integration, especially in Western Europe.

Nationalism was an important, but not the only, feature and not always the most conspicuous aspect of political and ideological change in Europe after the Cold War. Political ideas other than nationalism played an imperative role too. Especially in East-Central Europe and in the Baltic states, beliefs and aspirations concerning liberal democracy and human rights, economic progress and integration, and discussions about interdependence, international and European cooperation were at least as important as nationalist sentiments. During the late 1980s, the ideas of a 'Common European Home' and a 'Return to Europe' were guiding motives for reformist communist politicians such as Gorbachev, as well as for Central European dissident intellectuals.

And, especially in Western Europe, the political zeitgeist was initially evidently internationalist and 'millenarian optimist' [153: 140], rather than nationalist. The end of the Cold War, the defeat of communism in Europe and the unprecedentedly strong geopolitical and economic position of the 'West' invited a range of new ideas and beliefs on issues such as national sovereignty, humanitarian intervention and the general supremacy of liberal democracy and market economy, which translated into an expansionist liberal internationalism.

The internationalist spirit of the immediate post–Cold War years did not last long. The civil wars in the Balkans and the Caucasus and the stalled democratization and democratic reversals in various former communist countries challenged the liberal internationalist mood of the 1990s. Hegemonic optimism lost credibility because of the serious and persistent problems the 'international community' (read: the United States and its allies) encountered in the various places where they had intervened, in Iraq and Afghanistan but also in Bosnia-Herzegovina and Kosovo. The global financial crisis, the Eurozone crisis and the persistent economic malaise in the larger part of the European Union further weakened the West's sense of self-confidence.

One needs to go back in time more than half a millennium, to the fourteenth century perhaps, to find a map of Europe that resembles the political patchwork it represents today. Never before in history did Europe count more independent national states than it does now, in the first decade of the twenty-first century. During the early 1990s, Eastern Europe went through a process of unparalleled state disintegration and formation. The relevance of political nationalism in the collapse of old states and the building of new ones remains difficult to precisely estimate. The presence of a sense of common territorially based identity and solidarity may be a condition for separatism and for state formation, at least in modern European history, but it never seemed sufficient in isolation. Twice during the twentieth century Europe experienced 'waves' of state formation, after the First World War and after the Cold War. In both instances, nationalism was a major variable, but probably not the most important one. For an explanation of the timing and the development of the breakdown and the emergence of national states in Europe, nationalism was probably less important than the political manoeuvring of national and regional elites and the interventions by foreign powers.

So, it would be a misconception to see nationalism as the dominant or indeed the only politically relevant idea or ideology in post–Cold War Eastern Europe. Given the particularly deep social and economic problems that practically all countries suffered during the early stages of reform and considering the feeble position of many of the new political elites, radical political nationalism initially remained of remarkably limited importance in the mainstream politics of most countries in the former communist part of Europe. Additionally, the distinction between a predominantly civic or 'Western' and an ethnic or 'Eastern' variant of nationalism would also lose relevance – the latter became as much a part of the political discourse in Western Europe as the former inspired postcommunist intellectuals and politicians in Eastern Europe. During the 1990s, civic nationalism had an outspoken positive connotation in many former communist states. A strong national identity supposedly strengthened the political cohesion and loyalty that were considered as conditions for gaining national independence and sovereignty, and for building a new political and socio-economic order under very difficult circumstances. With the exception of Yugoslavia and parts of the former Soviet Union ethnically defined, exclusivist and intolerant nationalism generally remained limited. Only in former Yugoslavia were real or alleged ethnic differences manipulated, politicized and mobilized on such a scale that they led to massive violent conflict and ultimately to nationwide, fullscale civil war. In the former Soviet Union also, radical grass-roots and state-sponsored nationalism occurred, and not less dramatically for the people involved but on a smaller scale and mostly in the periphery of the empire, in the Caucasus and in Central Asia. Before discussing the Yugoslav Civil War and estimating the relevance of nationalism as a variable in the conflict in the Balkans, the political developments in post-communist Russia deserve attention.

Democratization and nationalism: the Russia case

The demise of communism and the fall of the Soviet Union occurred unexpectedly. While there was sufficient speculation about the stability of communism and the robustness of Soviet domination over Eastern Europe, it was only from the mid-1980s that the actual failure and disintegration of the Soviet empire was discussed as a real, not just a theoretical, possibility. Among the issues that were deemed of particular importance, the nationalities question reigned supreme. The French Russia specialist Hélène Carrère d'Encausse had been among the first to forecast the subversive impact of the nationalities issue on the durability of Soviet rule. In *L'Empire éclaté* ('The Collapsed Empire'), published 1978, she predicted that the Soviet Union would ultimately succumb to the inevitable revolt of its national minorities [28]. Carrère d'Encausse proved partly right and partly wrong. Nationalism and separatism played important roles in the fall of the Soviet Union, as previously discussed, but the critical issue was not the Muslim republics in Central Asia, as she initially predicted, but the proclamation of sovereignty by the Baltic states, by Ukraine and of course by Russia. After the leaders of the Soviet Union's three largest Slavic republics, Ukraine, Belarus and Russia, had signed the Belavezha Accords of 8 December 1991, thereby effectively dissolving the Soviet Union, the Central Asian communist leaderships practically begged to be included in the to-be-established Commonwealth of Independent States [136]. Apparently, the communist elites in Central Asia considered their interests better served by close and lasting ties with Russia than by full autonomy – about the same reason why half a year earlier they had supported the conservative coup against Gorbachev.

One of the major reasons that the disintegration of the Soviet Union occurred largely non-violently was its negotiated nature. Crucial political elites agreed to split up the country. The peaceful nature of the relations *between* most (former) Soviet republics was matched with mostly non-violent political struggle *within* the individual states. And the opposite was true as well: Soviet republics that had military conflicts with neighbouring countries frequently also faced violent disturbances within their own borders. Domestic change and foreign relations were intimately related, and nationalism seemed a crucial link. The political scientist Jack Snyder theorizes in *From Voting to Violence* (2000) how democratization and liberalization give often rise to warlike nationalism and violent domestic and international conflict [161]. During democratic transitions, ethnic political awareness peaks, while state power is still weak, Snyder argues. Additionally, in most democratizing countries, the 'political marketplace' tends to be imperfectly competitive and ethnically divided, whereby elites fight each other not constrained by forms of institutionalized control. In countries where the general population is poor, where democratic skills and experience are mostly lacking and where representative institutions, political parties and independent journalism remain weakly developed, nationalism can be expected to fill the void. Russia seemed an ideal candidate for Snyder's thesis. The country shared practically all of the characteristics that Snyder considered as conducive to nationalist conflict. However, a sober interpretation of early post-communist Russia suggests practically the opposite: it was the relative weakness rather than the strong presence of radical political nationalism that was one of the distinctive features of early post-communism in Russia (see also [109]).

After the collapse of communist rule, Russia lost its superpower status, its 'outer' and 'inner' empire, its international reputation and its confidence. Within a few years, Russia had lapsed from one of the world's two superpowers into a 'beggar state'. The country no longer instilled admiration or fear, as used to be the case during the Cold War, but a mere contempt and only a shimmer of sympathy. If Russia was still taken seriously, it was because of the dangerous weakness the country projected, not its strength. Seven decades of communist rule had left Russia's civil society in a dramatically underdeveloped state. This made civic politics, the wide popular trust and participation in a democratic polity, highly unlikely. Especially during the early years of post-communism, fragile democratic institutions coincided with what Snyder defined as a fairly open marketplace of ideas. Russia was still a relatively free country, with ample space for political engineers and adventurists. A beleaguered Yeltsin leadership was faced with an increasingly assertive opposition and an anxious and ever more frustrated population.

Russia's ethno-federal state structure also remained particularly prone to political manipulation on ethnic and nationalist grounds. Russia is partly organized, as was the Soviet Union, along ethno-federal lines. Many of Russia's more than 80 federal subjects are ethnically 'defined'. Ethno-federalism, as the late history of the Soviet empire had shown, tends to encourage the political use of ethnic themes and nationalist mobilization. After the collapse of the Soviet Union, approximately 25 million Russians (i.e., individuals who identified their nationality as Russian at the time of the 1989 census) suddenly found themselves beyond the borders of Russia. Practically overnight, they had switched status from a dominant nation in a multinational empire to an embattled minority in a foreign nation state. This minorities' issue offered a uniquely powerful tool for political mobilization and legitimation by any nationalist politician or ideologue in Moscow. It remains a kind of mystery why the struggling Yeltsin regime never seriously exploited it. It would take until the controversial presidential re-election of Vladimir Putin (in 2012), and the manifestation of political opposition that it caused, before the fate of the Russians beyond Russia became a prominent theme in official nationalist discourse.

Certainly, the former Soviet Union was the theatre of various nationalist conflicts. The first and the second Chechen Wars (1994–6, 1999–2000) were fought between Russia and separatist forces in the North Caucasus. Domestic politics and interregional relations between Georgia, Armenia and Azerbaijan were already poisoned by a venomous nationalism before the Soviet Union ceased to exist. This contributed to a range of related civil and international wars that would impact the region for decades to come. Georgians fought Ossetians and Abkhazians in the early 1990s, which initially led to a *de facto* and, after a brief war with Russia (August 2008), to a formal, independence of the two regions (although one could argue that Abkhazia and especially South Ossetia were actually incorporated into the Russian Federation). Armenia and Azerbaijan similarly fought a vicious war over Nagorno-Karabakh, which resulted in quasi-independence for the region, supported by Armenia, guarded by Russia and heavily contested by an increasingly wary and oil-rich Azerbaijan. The Russian Federation was directly involved in these and other conflicts (between Transnistria and Moldova proper, 1992, and in the civil war in Tajikistan, 1992–7) in the post-Soviet space, officially or informally, through the autonomous behaviour of local military commanders. Especially, Russia's second military campaign against Chechnya, around the time of Putin's election to the presidency in 2000, had many of the characteristics of a nationalist conflict in the context of the relationship between flawed democratization and war. While the immediate pre-history of the military campaign, including alleged terrorist attacks on civilian targets in some major Russian cities, still remains obscure, the war had all the properties of a case of unscrupulous political engineering. Among other things, it was a massive organized effort to raise the popularity and legitimacy of President-Elect Vladimir Putin.

Generally, however, the variant of nationalism as employed by Russia's leadership throughout most of the post-communist period was typically moderate and pragmatic. The distinction between civic and ethnic nationalisms has been nuanced earlier in this book, particularly where it denotes the dichotomy between a typically 'Western' versus an 'Eastern' variant of nationalism, but in Russia's case the difference seems not irrelevant. Historically, official nationalism in Russia is fashioned by the combination of a strong state, a weak society and an underdeveloped sense of national identity. State-sponsored nationalism traditionally served the creation of a supportive national identity, where the state, rather than the nation, was considered as the source of political power and legitimation. The Russian language has a word for this state-centred perspective: *gosudarstvennost* (literally: statism), from *gosudarstvo*, the state. Given that Russian nationalism traditionally emphasizes the state rather than the nation, it generally targets the citizens of Russia, the earlier-mentioned *Rossiiskie*, rather than the ethnic Russians, the *Russkie*. With some exceptions, such as the anti-Semitic propaganda during late Tsarist and Stalinist times, official nationalism in Russia remained primarily civic – irrespective of the political nature of the regime. The multi-ethnic composition of the Russian empire and state, population and elite rendered nation building based on ethnic criteria dangerous. Ethnic nationalism would be inevitably divisive and disintegrative. After 1917, communist ideological considerations would create additional difficulties for the definition of an ethnic Russian national identity.

It is no exaggeration to claim that in the early 1990s, Boris Yeltsin was carried into the Kremlin on a wave of Russian national enthusiasm. Although Russia's declaration of sovereignty was never subjected to a popular referendum, it was almost certainly widely supported in society, based on the earlier-mentioned belief that Russians had been victimized by communist rule as much, if not more, than the other Soviet nations. While the Yeltsin leadership used the national victimization argument freely, its nationalism remained typically defensive rather than expansive. Yeltsin probably had reason to fear that the further mobilization of Russian nationalism under the difficult conditions of post-communism could rekindle sentiments that were difficult to control and therefore potentially detrimental for his rule. On the other hand, it may also have been the often-perceived weakness of the Russians' national identity that persuaded the Yeltsin leadership to mostly abstain from nationalist engineering. In 1996, Yeltsi even decided to appoint a committee of specialists to elaborate on the national identity of the Russian people, and to work out an effective definition of 'Russianness'. '[A]ll that would be funny, if it were not so sad', as the historian of Russian national identity Nicholas Riasanovsky [142: 231] later mused.

More than two decades into the post-communist era, it seems legitimate to question whether the variables that have produced the predominantly moderate and civic form of official nationalism in Russia still count. After almost a generation of economic and political recovery, Russia's ruling elite has secured its power. It has significantly strengthened its hold over society, consolidated the authority of the state and strengthened the country's global position. To be sure, nationalism has always been part of Russian politics. At every election, millions of Russians have voted for the Communist Party of the Russian Federation, which combines Marxism-Leninism with Russian nationalism, or for the Liberal Democratic Party of Vladimir Zhirinovsky. Anti-immigration is a particularly widespread sentiment among Russians, and violence against foreigners, especially Asians and individuals from the Caucasus, is the order of the day. But particularly since Putin's third presidential term, from 2012, and the popular protests that it triggered, official nationalism also seems to have sharpened and radicalized. The Russian leadership generously employed political rhetoric (Putin as the 'national leader') and organizations (the official youth organization Nashi, 'Ours', and other quasi-autonomous institutions) with ever-stronger nationalistic connotations. This more pronounced Russian nationalism seemed part of a conservative ideological turn by the Putin leadership, emphasizing Russia's unique national identity against the perceived materialism and moral emptiness of the 'West'. The discourse of Russian nationalism radicalized again significantly during and after the Crimean crisis, in the spring of 2014, when it acquired an explicitly geopolitical and ever-stronger anti-Western dimension, reminding many of the days of the Cold War. Putin openly deplored the weakness of Russia's national identity. He considered it as a political liability. Russia needs 'to preserve [its] identity in a rapidly changing world, a world that has become more open, transparent, and interdependent', the president emphasized at a meeting between Russia specialists, in September 2013. '[I]t is impossible to move forward without spiritual, cultural and national self-determination.' But Putin also remained largely true to the traditional civic nature of Russian nationalism. 'Nationalists must remember that Russia was formed specifically as a multi-ethnic and multi-confessional country from its very inception', he emphasized. 'Nationalists must remember that by calling into question our multi-ethnic character, and exploiting the issue of Russian, Tatar, Caucasian, Siberian or any other nationalism or separatism, means that we are starting to destroy our genetic code. In effect', as Putin concluded, 'we will begin to destroy ourselves' [138].

Resurgent nationalism in Russia under the third presidency of Vladimir Putin is mostly understood as an instrument to acquire political legitimacy by an increasingly unpopular regime, given its apparent lack of other powerful ideological or normative alternatives [68]. Others consider the emergence of nationalism under Putin mainly as a matter of catching up. Nationalism in Russia 'does not merely spell extremism, marginalization, radicalism, or opposition to power', Marlene Laruelle [105: 2] concluded well before the Crimea crisis, 'but in actual fact [it] marks a return to ... normalcy' (see also [104]). Regardless of how one interprets the resurgence of nationalism in Putin's Russia, it does little to alter one of the most remarkable differences between Russia and early post-communist Yugoslavia. Different from the multinational Soviet Union, in the state of the South Slavs, political nationalism would play a crucially important and an utterly destructive role.

Civil war in Yugoslavia

While the disintegration of the Soviet Union and its outer empire was historically peaceful, the collapse of Yugoslavia, that other multinational communist state, led to a series of civil wars that lasted into the next decade. More than 100,000 people perished during the conflicts. Two million people were driven from their homes, as cities and regions were 'ethnically cleansed'. Bosnian Serb troops led by General Ratko Mladić committed mass murder after the capture of the enclave of Srebrenica (July 1995). In four days and within earshot of Dutch UN soldiers, more than 7,000 Muslim boys and men were apparently killed. It was a war crime, noted Tony

Judt, similar to those in Oradour, Lidice and Katyń during the Second World War [87: 678].[1]

The break-up of Yugoslavia and the large-scale violence that followed have been interpreted in two distinct ways. The first explanation stresses the historical and ethnic dimensions of the conflict. The second interpretation emphasizes the actual political dynamics of Yugoslavia's collapse and civil wars. All studies of the origins and the development of the war stress the crucial role of political nationalism.

In the first explanation, the separatist wars in Yugoslavia are understood as the latest episode in a long history of mutual antagonism and conflict between the major ethnic groups in the region. Mutual violence, war and instability were supposedly fixed ingredients in the history of the Balkans. The wars of the 1990s should be seen as merely the latest episode in a long historical line of internecine aggression. This interpretation strongly echoes Kohn's distinction between ethnic and civic nationalism. Ethnic nationalism looks backward, as Kohn [97: 574] already wrote. It is 'founded on history, on monuments and graveyards'. This line of thought would be regularly repeated during the Yugoslav Civil War. *Balkan Ghosts* by the American journalist Robert D. Kaplan [92] was probably the most well known and certainly the most influential example of this primordial interpretation of the war. The book supposedly informed the position of the American President Bill Clinton (1993–2001). One of the reasons why Kaplan's interpretation proved so popular was because it made it intellectually possible to lift the war out of the current European/Western reality. The ethnic dimension of

---

[1] In the spring of 1940, in Katyń and other places in the Belarusian part of the former Soviet Union, the Soviet secret police executed more than 20,000 Polish nationals, including many military and police officers. The mass graves were discovered by German troops in late 1942 and early 1943. The Soviet regime denied any involvement. Only after the collapse of the Soviet Union, in 1991, did Moscow confirm Soviet responsibility for the massacres.

On 10 June 1944, the SS Panzer Division Das Reich murdered almost the entire population of the French village of Oradour-sur-Glane. It was an act of retaliation for an attack by the resistance shortly before in a neighbouring village, in which some German soldiers were killed. The extermination of the population of the Czech town Lidice was a German revenge for the attack on 27 May 1942 on the highly placed Nazi Reinhard Heydrich, governor of the Protectorate of Bohemia and Moravia.

the Yugoslav Civil War gave it an essentially pre-modern and non-European distinctiveness. Apart from the biased interpretation of the Balkans' past and the inclination to read history backwards, this explanation missed the crucial question of timing: why and how were the Yugoslavs suddenly engulfed by radically nationalist sentiments?

Most scholars, both experts on nationalism and area specialists, present more nuanced views [56; 152; 157; 183]. Their explanations often combine aspects of the ethnic and of the political explanation. They accept the enduring relevance of historic antagonisms among the South Slavs as an important variable of the conflict, but they consider the manipulation and mobilization of these resentments, in a situation of political and economic change and uncertainty, as the explanation of the particularly vicious nature of these wars.

There is no doubt that historical memories and resentments centred on ethnic identities played a crucial role in the disintegration and the violent collapse of communist Yugoslavia. The atrocities that were committed during the 1990s were certainly inspired by the memory of the conflicts of the recent past, particularly during the Second World War, and by the deep mutual distrust that these had aroused. However, wars never break out spontaneously, not even in the Balkans. The Yugoslav wars of succession cannot be explained by ethnic animosity or a history of conflict only. For an understanding of the falling apart of Yugoslavia and of the wars that were fought on its territory, an insight into the political motives and behaviour of the (post-)Yugoslav elites is crucial. This 'political' explanation of the civil war was articulately presented by the American representative in the international negotiations which would eventually bring the armed conflict to an end, Ambassador Richard Holbrooke [73]. Holbrooke, and others, nuanced the relevance of historical conflict and ethnic animosity as explanatory variables, and focused mainly on the interests and ambitions of the political elites. Their main argument is that Yugoslavia's republican leaderships had a keen interest in either the break-up of the country, which applied particularly to the Croatian and Slovenian leadership, or in its continuation under their own authority, which pertained to the Serbian political elite under Slobodan Milošević in Belgrade. In this explanation, nationalism is the exceptionally effective tool of political manipulation and mobilization, which Breuilly

[16] mentions in his historical analyses and others, as Snyder [161] and Mann [112, 113] in their democratization-nationalist conflict thesis.

Among the Serbian elites, Slobodan Milošević was the crucial individual. Milošević made a career in business, in the banking sector, before he became president of the Socialist Republic of Serbia (1989) and after the collapse of communist Yugoslavia of the Federal Republic of Yugoslavia (in 1997). Milošević acquired national fame when in April 1987 he spoke at a gathering of fellow Serbs and Montenegrins on the Field of Blackbirds. 'No one has the right to beat you', he promised his audience, among whom were mostly Serbian victims of earlier clashes with the local Kosovo-Albanian police. These simple words, spoken by a visibly nervous, Milošević, were an unmistakable reference to the growing tensions between Serbs and Kosovar-Albanians, and to the developing Serbian national awareness. The Field of Blackbirds has mythical significance in Serbia. It is a crucially important aspect of the nation's collective memory. In June 1389, on the Field of Blackbirds, a Serbian army suffered a heroic defeat by the advancing Ottomans. It meant the end of Serbia's medieval kingdom and the beginning of more than 500 years of Turkish rule. This is the preferred commemoration. In historical reality, it was a multinational military force that awaited the Turks, and the battle ended in a devastating draw after both armies had been practically wiped out. More relevant, however, than the precise outcome of the battle was its location. The Field of Blackbirds is also known as Kosovo *Polje*, or field, in today's independent Kosovo. An impressive monument on Kosovo Polje memorializes the historical battle, more the half a millennium ago. The site has been under long-term protection by international peacekeepers.

Milošević was the archetypical communist-turned-nationalist. Leading up to the Yugoslav conflict, he acted as more communist leaders did. To continue their profitable positions of power, they used radical nationalist rhetoric as a compensation for the erosion of communist ideology. Milošević was far from the only individual responsible for the collapse of Yugoslavia and the massive violence that ensued. He shared the blame with his Croatian counterpart Franjo Tuđman (1990–9) and with a range of other military men, politicians and public intellectuals in most of the country's constituent republics. The policies of Milošević, Tuđman and others point to an important variable of political change during the turbulent 1990s in Eastern Europe, that is, the role and relevance of political individuals. 'Agency' is crucial to the stark difference between the relatively peaceful fragmentation of the Soviet Union and the terribly violent collapse of Yugoslavia. Time makes the man, but sometimes man (or woman) makes the time too. Individuals matter in periods of change and insecurity. The antagonisms between population groups in the Soviet Union may have generally been less virulent than in Yugoslavia. Relations between Russians and the other Soviet 'nations' were probably less conflictive than those between Serbs and other South Slavs. However, apart from these and other structural aspects, it was mostly agency, or the behaviour of individual politicians, that made the essential difference. If Milošević and Tudman would have shown a bit more of the hesitation, the wavering, if not the personal morality of Mikhail Gorbachev, the break-up of Yugoslavia might have been a much less violent, less vicious episode in the recent history of the Balkans.

Nationalism not only manifested itself in the eastern part of Europe; it also returned to Western Europe. Western Europe may not have gone through the same dramatic transformation as the former communist part of the continent, but also in the West of Europe the end of the Cold War meant the end of a historical episode. The collapse of communism and the disintegration of the Soviet Union and its sphere of influence questioned many of the geopolitical certainties of the last half century. It allowed for the eastward enlargement of NATO, the European Union and other institutions, thereby effectively terminating the geopolitical meaning of 'Western Europe' as it had been known. But more important was the acceleration of changes that predated the end of the Cold War. Earlier than most other parts of the world, the highly developed countries of Western Europe were impacted by what became generally known as globalization, by the increasing cross-border links between states, economies and societies through trade and investment flows, migration and new global information and communication technologies. Among the more conspicuous effects was the re-emergence of nationalism and national identity as prominent, everyday political notions. Nationalism returned to Western Europe both in its civic and in its ethnic variant.

Globalization, integration and the nation state

Economic and cultural globalization and European integration
had a paradoxical impact on the nations and states of Europe. They
levelled and they encouraged national differences. They made societies more alike, and, as a result, they also triggered an interest in
specifically national, ethnic, cultural, even political distinctiveness.
Globalization and integration generated a new 'politics of identity'.
Anthony Smith [157: 3] quizzed the apparent paradox between the
resurgence of nationalism, religious fundamentalism and ethnic
conflict in a world that seemed to become ever smaller:

> Is it an inevitable product of a dialectic or cultural globalization
> which produces a new kind of identity politics in the wake of
> the disembedding revolution of modernity, or just a 'survival'
> from an earlier age of nationalist hatreds and wars? Is it simply a
> temporary aberration, which further capitalist or post-industrial
> progress will iron out in area after area? Or is this contradiction
> of modern culture likely to grow and intensify as it spreads across
> the globe?

Smith suggested three answers. First, the current (1990s) wave
of nationalism was a survival from another epoch, an ephemeral
phenomenon that would eventually pass away. Second, post–Cold
War nationalism was the answer to the unprecedented changes of
our times, to the disruptive, alienating effects of the latest wave of
economic and technological globalization. Third, late-twentieth-
century nationalist conflict was neither the remainder of earlier
epochs of nationalism nor the unfortunate by-product of modernity.
Nationalism was never absent. Nations remained the 'bedrock of
human society'. Nationalism was perennial. Smith's own conclusion
was a combination of the three arguments. In his understanding, the
complexity of nations and nationalism could only be understood by
contextualizing them in a wider time frame and in different spaces –
history, territory and ethnicity. Any attempt to grasp the trends of
globalism and its paradoxical effect, the new 'localism', must therefore relate them not merely to processes of modernization, but also
to earlier pre-modern identities and legacies that continue to form
the foundation of many modern nations [157: 1–6, 47]. It is precisely at the intermediate level of the national state, Smith argues,
that globalization had its largest impact [159: 148].

Among the most significant changes in post–Cold War Europe was the perceived decline of the national state. The changing nature and relevance of the state generated a huge scholarly debate. The crisis of the nation state thesis was controversial, but also widely shared, especially during the 1990s [33; 162; 173]. Most analyses focused on the growing discrepancy between an increasingly globalized economic and financial infrastructure versus a still predominantly national organization of political life. The traditional, strictly geographical manner in which we had organized our modern polities, the national state, proved ever less consistent with the dynamics of modern economy and society, neither hindered nor determined by political boundaries. How serious was the crisis of the national state? 'Very serious', wrote the British political scientist William Wallace in the mid-1990s. The nation state was in undeniable retreat. With a reference to the Maastricht Treaty (1992), he asserted that all crucial functions of the national state were affected by European integration:

> control of the national territory and borders, police, citizenship and immigration, currency, taxation, financial transfers, management of the economy, promotion of industry, representation and accountability, also foreign policy and defence. [173: 65–6]

Wallace observed a growing disconnect between nation and state, as borders became more porous, ethnic diversity more obvious, national myths less convincing and individuals more autonomous [173: 45]. The historian Mark Mazower took the argument a few steps further. While social problems and alienation grew, Europe's nation states were gradually reduced to 'mere shells', he argued [117: 359].

With hindsight, the idea of the decline of the national state needs serious qualification. The 'crisis of the nation state' was probably more a reflection of the internationalist, if not universalist, zeitgeist of the 1990s than a representation of what had really changed. To begin with, the sovereignty and competences of the national state in Europe have always been subjected to formal and informal limitations, during and after the Cold War. The idea that national states have ever been fully autonomous or sovereign is a fallacy, a form of 'organized hypocrisy' [100: 69]. One could additionally argue that from the late twentieth century, the power and influence by the state over the citizen rather increased than decreased. The democratic government today knows more about its individual citizens than yesterday's totalitarian leaders could ever have dreamed. And finally, whereas the competence and relevance of the national state in Europe have waned in some spheres, they have increased in others. This may apply particularly to the state's role in providing physical and social security, due respectively to the emergence of international terrorism and civil conflict throughout large parts of the world, and to the socio-economic consequence of the forces of globalization and integration.

The post–Cold War development of the welfare state offers an interesting case of how the 'national' continues to reign supreme over the 'international'. The welfare state is supposed to be a closed arrangement, limited only to the citizens of a given state. The sustainability of the national welfare state is increasingly questioned, however. The growing heterogeneity and open nature of modern society seriously challenge the three pillars of the welfare state: political choice, financial feasibility and common solidarity. A possible answer to the predicament of the welfare state is to further 'Europeanize' welfare, to lift it to the level of the European Union. This however has proven extremely controversial, and practically impossible [53]. Social welfare remains a most vital prerogative (and legitimating argument) of the national state, and deepening European integration has rather strengthened this claim. The image of a 'neoliberal Europe' has become a staple of Euroscepticism. Many people have come to regard the European Union as a threat rather than a support to the provisions of the welfare state.

Two major features of European integration seem particularly at odds with the fundamentals of the national welfare state. Over the last couple of decades, the European Union has become culturally and socio-economically more diverse, which makes it increasingly difficult to recognize the 'other' with whom citizens share the fruits and burdens of cooperation. The growing diversity of an ever-larger 'Europe' arguably undermines the sense of communality, solidarity and trust that is crucial to the legitimacy of the welfare regime [102; 114]. Moreover, citizens also need to feel a common allegiance to the decision-making and distributive institutions of the welfare state. This too proves difficult in the case of Europe. The complex, multi-layered and contested European 'polity' is often perceived as insufficiently transparent, democratic and accountable.

More than anything else perhaps, the national state survived as the focus of political identity and loyalty for most of its citizens. It is difficult to measure and impossible to prove, but national identity seemed to have grown stronger rather than weaker in Europe after the Cold War. This looks evident for the millions of Europeans who have established their independent nation state after the demise of the communist multinational states, but it may also apply to many of the citizens of the 'old' nation states in Western Europe. The competitors of national identity are still few. Internationalist political ideologies are either dead (communism) or they have never really trumped national identity (social democracy). Religion may have become a transnational marker of political identity and affiliation for a growing number of citizens, especially Muslim immigrants, but as yet they form a minority among Europeans. Another potential alternative to national identity, 'Europeanism', seems to have made even less progress. To be sure, identity is not a one-dimensional phenomenon. It is changeable and diverse. Individuals can have multiple political identities. One may feel particular commitment to a political party, to the national state and to Europe simultaneously. In that case, an individual's identity is inclusive, rather than exclusive. But even in the case of these multiple and inclusive identities, very few Europeans would argue that they feel primary allegiance to Europe, or to the European Union, rather than to their own national state.

The failure of the European Union to make much inroad into these core issues of national welfare and identity stands in contrast with the overall advance of integration after the Cold War. From the 1990s, the European Union succeeded in achieving both substantial widening and deepening. In 2004 and 2007, ten former communist countries entered the union. This officially concluded more than a decade of structural reforms in these countries, guided by the so-called Copenhagen criteria for accession to the Union. No other outside power, with the exception of an occupying state, had ever exercised a deeper influence on countries' sovereign domestic affairs than the European Union had on these East-Central European states. But eastward enlargement would also strongly impact the European Union itself, especially its organizational and administrative structures. The European Union became increasingly diverse, and its decision-making process complex and burdensome. The European Union became an institution of varied membership and multi-speeds. But more than anything else, the process of enlargement seemed to have affected the longer-term legitimacy of European integration.

With the Maastricht Treaty, signed in 1992, the European Community turned into a Union. The Economic and Monetary Union (EMU) was agreed upon, which offered the framework for the introduction of a European currency, the euro. The EMU came into force on 1 January 1999. Eleven countries introduced the euro, thereby giving up one of the most historic and evocative aspects and symbols of national identity and sovereignty: their national currency. While the decision to abandon the national currency was understandably difficult and controversial in most countries, the actual introduction of the euro went remarkably smoothly. With hindsight, it probably even went too smoothly. A decade later, from 2009, the Eurozone's financial crisis would starkly expose the flaws of the EMU. The political imperative to construct a common currency had evidently trumped sound economic and monetary considerations.

In October 2004, well before the global financial crisis came into view, the European heads of government and the French president took another major step forward and signed a draft European Constitution. It was a unique document, agreed at a time of great European optimism and generally seen as a milestone event in the European integration process – however, it proved to be dramatically short-lived. The ratification of the European Constitution differed from country to country. In most member states, simple parliamentarian majorities sanctioned the document. In Spain, Luxembourg, France and the Netherlands, though, the draft constitution was submitted to a referendum. In the first two countries, the proposal was adopted by a substantial majority of respectively 76.7 and 56.5 per cent of the vote. In the latter two, however, the draft constitution was decidedly rejected. To the surprise and the utter dismay of the generally pro-European political and societal elites, not to mention the bureaucracy in Brussels, only 45.1 per cent of the French electorate (in May 2005) and 38.5 per cent of the Dutch voters (in June 2005) supported the constitutional document. The effort to create a European Constitution was crushed. The French and Dutch 'no' were certainly not only inspired by anti-European or crude nationalist sentiments. The unpopularity of the incumbent president and government and the rather unsophisticated campaign by the supporters of the constitution also played an important role. But the outcome of the referendums *did* show how widely Euroscepticism had meanwhile spread in the two founding states. Whether it was the neoliberal image of the European Union that had aroused antipathy, the seemingly unstoppable process of deepening and widening integration or the perceived costly nature of the Brussels bureaucracy, the bottom line was the same: the further development of European integration was widely perceived to be at odds with the interests of the nation and the national state. Issues such as the national interest, even national identity, had firmly re-entered the political debate on European integration.

Enlargement, the euro, but also the Treaty of Lisbon, as the European Constitution became known after a two-year 'period of reflection', were testaments to the dynamics of the integration process. The first two post–Cold War decades were among the most energetic phases of progress in the history of European integration. But under the surface and not yet appreciated by the larger part of the political and administrative elite, things were changing. Inspired by feelings of unease and insecurity among a significant part of the population, European integration gradually became a real political issue. In 2008, the political scientists Liesbet Hooghe and Gary Marks published a landmark article which captured the essence of these changes. They argued that from the 1990s the 'permissive consensuses' which had allowed national and European political elites to advance European integration without much popular interest and scrutiny had gradually changed into 'constraining dissension', which put clear limitations on the elites' freedom to manoeuvre, as a result of growing popular and political attention and scepticism [74: 5]. Political discussion and competition over an ever larger and more diverse European Union became increasingly about 'who one is', rather than 'what one gets', Hooghe and Marks argued. The debate on Europe transcended traditional party lines and entered the realm of identity politics [74: 12, 16].

Given the scope of the integration, the degree of cooperation between countries of different sizes and weights as well as the extent of the Union's prerogatives over its member states, the elitist nature of the integration process had had clear political advantages. It enabled the political class to expand and deepen the integration process in an almost undisturbed manner. 'The EU's greatest tactical advantage is that it is, in a word, so boring', wrote Moravcsik [123: 238] about the relative ease with which the Union rebounded after the French and Dutch had rejected the constitution. But the elitist or stealthy nature of European cooperation also had its drawbacks. It hid the feelings of scepticism among many citizens. The peoples of Europe were not often invited to express their opinion on European integration. But when they were asked, their response was oftentimes negative.

Generally, European integration raised more popular support in countries about to enter the union than in countries which already enjoyed membership. Practically all referendums on membership resulted in a positive outcome. Norway remains a stark exception. Both in 1972 and again in 1994, the Norwegian population rejected entry into the European Community. Relatedly, and with exceptions again, polls on specific Europe-related issues such as introducing the euro or accepting the European Constitution relatively often showed negative results. In June 1992, the Danish electorate rejected the Maastricht Treaty. In 2000, the Danes again overruled the introduction of the euro. In 1995 the French and the Dutch vetoed the Constitution, and a few years later the Irish would reject its successor document, the Treaty of Lisbon. But the most important inference from all Euro referendums[2] seems to be the gap between the level of 'Europeanism' among the governments and other elites and that of the populations at large. The latter are unequivocally more sceptical about Europe than the former. Support for European integration also appears to have a pronounced sociological dimension. Voting behaviour seems strongly influenced by social status and income. Individuals lower on the social ladder are generally more sceptical about Europe than individuals higher up. It is another dimension of the elitist image and reality of European integration.

While it seems safe to assume that a majority of Europeans have always supported the idea of European integration as well as being part of it, enthusiasm for the form integration has actually taken, that is the European Union in its current shape, is less assured, and probably under increasing pressure.[3] European integration is

---

[2] For a full list of Euro referendums, see http://en.wikipedia.org/wiki/Referendums_related_to_the_European_Union.

[3] Public opinion on European integration and related issues is polled on an almost permanent basis. Check the Pew Research Center (www.pewresearch.org) and the EU's Eurostat websites (http://ec.europa.eu/public_opinion/index_en.htm) for updated information.

often seen as too costly and too complex. The European Union is considered as a behemoth, which instils feelings of estrangement and alienation rather than sympathy or support. It has become too big, too complex, too overpowering.

Euroscepticism is an important aspect of the 'constraining dissension' by Hooghe and Marks. It illustrates particularly well the growing politicization of European integration. Euroscepticism comes in different forms and shapes, in a similar manner to but not automatically identical with political nationalism. The reserved reactions to initiatives such as the Maastricht Treaty or the Constitution especially expressed the reluctance to grant more power to European institutions. The hesitancy to transfer prerogatives from the national to the European level can be inspired by multiple considerations. The argument that the nation is by definition the right unit of government could indeed be considered as a 'nationalist assumption' [5: 44], but the belief that 'Europe' is too non-transparent and too undemocratic to be endowed with so much power might also reflect fully different political orientations. What both arguments do have in common, though, is a firm dose of Euroscepticism. Euroscepticism is a variegated phenomenon, which stands in a complex relationship to nationalism. The moderate variant of Euroscepticism expresses serious doubts and concerns about the nature of the integration process. The radical variant, also known as anti-Europeanism, opposes the very idea and the whole practice of European integration. This difference has also been defined as 'soft' and 'hard' Euroscepticism [165] or, slightly different, as 'diffuse' and 'specific' Euroscepticism [98]. Moderate or soft Euroscepticism manifests itself through mainstream or centrist parties. Radical, sometimes extremist, political parties, from both the right and the left, mostly voice hard or specific Euroscepticism.

Post–Cold War Europe saw the emergence of a range of new Eurosceptical parties. During the 2000s especially, radically Eurosceptic or anti-EU parties made considerable inroads into a series of member states. The Party for Freedom in the Netherlands won 15.5 percent of the popular vote in the parliamentary elections of 2010. For two years, the party formally supported a coalition government of Christian Democrats and Liberals. The party is in favour of a Dutch exit from the European Union. In Finland, the 'True Finns' party gathered more than 19 per cent of the popular vote in 2011. In crisis-ridden Greece, Euroscepticism of both variants exploded. Syriza, which was critical of the EU-imposed austerity measures rather than of membership *per se*, won more than 36 per cent in the January 2015 general elections. In other countries, less extremist parties also campaigned on Eurosceptical platforms. In Italy, Berlusconi's Popolo della Libertà (The People of Freedom) and the Movimento 5 Stelle (Five Star Movement) of Beppe Grillo won more than 40 per cent of the popular vote in the early 2013 elections. Growing popular hesitations about European integration in France strongly benefited the Front National. Marine Le Pen's party scored more than 13 per cent in the first round of the elections for the Assemblée Nationale and 14.9 per cent during the presidential elections of 2012.

Eurosceptical ideas run along political and national lines. Especially since the Eurozone crisis, Eurosceptical arguments are no longer aimed exclusively at the European Union, which many Europeans consider to be at least partially responsible for the depth and duration of the crisis, but also against other member states. The Greeks' anger and frustration with the position of the German government became extremely nasty, including references to the Nazi past and the Second World War. Among the crisis's creditor nations in the northern Eurozone (Germany, Finland, the Netherlands, Austria), financial assistance to the debtor states was mostly sold to the electorates as being in the long-term self-interest, rather than as an act of solidarity with fellow member states in a crisis. Governments stressed the 'cold' transactional nature of their financial assistance. The element of reciprocity involved was the firm condition imposed on the debtor states in the south (Greece, Italy, Portugal, Spain and Ireland) that they would realize a programme of financial austerity and structural economic and administrative reforms, including, in some cases, a change of government to one which would be more 'Euro-compatible'. What creditor countries considered as reasonable and sensible demands for long-foregone reforms, many in the debtor countries saw as acts of foreign arrogance and intervention. Perceptions of the national interest have become increasingly diversified in the Eurozone.

Why did European integration trigger varieties of Euroscepticism, and why did it never produce the 'mirror image' of a common and widely shared European identity? The essence of the answer probably is that European integration, whether thriving or waning, never succeeded in significantly reducing the relevance of the national state as the major focus of political loyalty. Most Europeans continue to identify primarily or even exclusively with their own nation, region or state, rather than with 'Europe', and even less with the European Union. Europe has its own flag, anthem, its own 'Europe Day', but it failed to establish a deep sense of European identity and solidarity among a majority of its citizens. Why has the spillover effect of European integration never reached the realm of identity? An obvious answer to the question is a follow-up question: what would the nature of such a European identity be? Europe never had a distinctive common language, religion, popular culture or history. The European Union's *self*-identity has never had a deep impact on the general population. What the European Union claims as its essential achievements are either widely accepted as obvious (peace) or they are not attributed to the European Union but rather to the national state (welfare, democracy, human rights). As with every national identity, the European identity has been 'constructed' in contradistinction to important 'others'. But Europe's major other has been its own past, the long history of divisive nationalism, mutual conflict and war. For many Europeans today, used to the peaceful conditions of their part of the continent, that same history does not seem to have adequate legitimating power anymore. And even if peace on the European continent is no longer taken for granted under current conditions, the European Union is not widely considered as the institution that guarantees it.

Migration, multiculturalism and political nationalism

Political nationalism in post–Cold War Europe was mainly fuelled by two developments: European integration and immigration. Migration in Europe increased substantially after the Cold War, both between European countries and from outside Europe into the European Union. Citizens of EU member states have the legal right to live and work in other member states. Following eastward enlargement, it was mostly citizens of the new Eastern European member states who sought work outside of their own countries. The Eurozone crisis initiated another, limited migration flow from the member states in crisis to the countries with economies that continued to flourish, especially Germany. Various member states of the

European Union applied temporary restrictions on working permits within their borders for Eastern Europeans, especially Poles, Romanians and Bulgarians. The United Kingdom waived restrictions on foreign labour, and it received more than half a million Poles during the first years after Eastern enlargement. Apart from labour migration from within Europe, increasing numbers of asylum seekers reached the countries of the European Union, initially from the Balkans, then later from crisis areas in the Middle East and Africa.

In Western Europe, the politically contentious nature of the minorities issue has emerged relatively recently. It is linked to migration waves that do not go back more than three or four decades, and it became especially poignant only after the Cold War. The public debate focuses on Muslim immigrants and their perceived reluctance to integrate and assimilate. In Eastern Europe, the minorities' issue is mostly concentrated around 'historical' minorities, population groups that are generally as strongly rooted in the country or region as the ethnic majority. Ethnic and political lines often run parallel in East-Central Europe. Whereas party formation on the basis of ethnicity is still relatively uncommon in Western Europe, it occurred frequently in the post-communist world, especially in the early phase of transition. The Dvizhenie za Prava i Svobodi (Movement for Rights and Freedoms) in Bulgaria, the Partia Demokratike Shqiptare (Democratic Party of Albanians) in Macedonia and the Romániai Magyar Demokrata Szövetség (Democratic Union of Hungarians in Romania) are prime examples of ethnically based political parties. Although few specific data are available on the national make-up of political parties and their supporters, it seems reasonable to suggest that, on the whole, ethnicity as a basis for party formation has gradually become less noticeable in the former communist countries. The minority issue itself seemed to have lost potency. The processes of political and economic change that have preceded and followed the accession to the European Union took away most of its political virulence. Among the main exceptions are the countries further to the east in Europe, that have no accession perspective, such as the Ukraine and Georgia, and some of the former republics of Yugoslavia, particularly the regions that have been under international administration, such as Bosnia-Herzegovina from 1995 and Kosovo from 2000. In these countries, military intervention and foreign administration have led to the cessation of brutal civil wars, but the reconciliation of the different population groups still seems a distant dream. Despite all efforts by the international community, and especially the European Union, these countries' societies and political landscapes have remained sharply ethnically segmented. Apart from the Western Balkans, multiple former Soviet republics also continued to struggle with minorities' issues, often perceived as 'national' or 'ethnic' conflicts. In 2014, a politically and ethnically divided Ukraine, insofar as the Russian-speaking part of the population in the eastern regions of the country is indeed 'ethnically' different from their fellow citizens, would become the theatre of bloody civil strife and the most serious international conflict since the end of the Cold War. Especially the Crimean Peninsula triggered the revisionist interest of the Russian leadership. The Crimea was the only part of Ukraine where 'Russians' were in a majority. Soviet leader Nikita Khrushchev (1953–64) had formally transferred Crimea from the Russian to the Ukrainian part of the Soviet Union in 1954. In the summer of 1991, it became part of independent Ukraine after the republic had declared independence. While Crimea retained a special status within the Ukraine and enjoyed extensive autonomy, it also continued to be a contentious issue in the bilateral relations between the Ukraine and its large neighbour in the east. In the spring of 2014, relations between Russia and the Ukraine suddenly and dramatically worsened. Russian President Vladimir Putin refused to accept the collapse of his political ally in the Ukraine, the Yanukovich regime, and the abrupt turn westwards of its successor government. He responded by a *de facto* military occupation of Crimea and its formal reintegration into the Russian Federation.

Different from their fellow men in the Ukraine, including Crimea, after 1991, Russian minorities in the Baltic states, especially Estonia and Latvia, continued to feel disadvantaged and discriminated against in their new home countries. In the two republics, exclusivist legislation was introduced, which linked citizenship to ethnic belonging, thereby effectively reducing substantial Russian minorities to second-class citizens. Eager to eliminate the vestiges of 40 years of Soviet rule, the governments in the Baltic states insisted on the creation of a strong and legally supported mono-national identity, the impact of which was particularly felt of course by the former 'dominant' population groups, the Russians and other Russian speakers.

A considerable part of the Russian minority remained effectively stateless, suffering the uncertain position of non-permanent residence. While their less-than-equal situation did not persuade ethnic Russians or other minorities to leave these countries in large numbers, it did create a enduring sense of unease and frustration, which occasionally erupted into violent confrontations with the authorities. One of the most symbolic incidents took place in April 2007, when the Estonian government decided to remove a bronze statue of a Soviet soldier from the centre of Tallinn to a park on its outskirts. The act triggered a vehement protest on the part of the Russian population and led to two days of rioting between angry Russian youngsters and the police. One person died, a hundred were wounded, and more than a thousand were arrested.

Post–Cold War Europe struggles with two different 'minority issues': 'old' and 'new' minorities, territorially bound or sub-state regionalism and immigration. Sub-state regionalism entails a shifting of political identity and loyalty from the national state to one's own region. In many countries, this kind of nationalism is deeply rooted in the history of specific regions and their inhabitants. It is enjoyed by minorities among the general population, who often are majorities within their own part of the country. Regionalism becomes politically critical when these minorities no longer share the identity and solidarity that is minimally required to live together in one national state. The forms, ambitions and political relevance of regionalism in Europe varied widely in post-war history. Regionalism could be peaceful and it could be violent. As a political ambition, regionalism could recognize the legitimacy of the national and strive for sub-state autonomy, or it could deny it, and aim for separatism and full independence. It was this radical variant of regionalism, in effect a variety of nationalism, which required particular relevance in the communist part of Europe. The disintegration of Yugoslavia and the former Soviet Union enabled multiple national minorities to realize their political ambition of independence, thereby eliminating an important undercurrent of frustration and instability in post-war Europe. But drawing new borders almost always implied the creation of new minorities. Many of the newly independent states were formed along ethnic lines of division, but most remained far from ethnically homogeneous. New frontiers created new cross-border minorities, and new conflicts erupted between population groups in Bosnia, Kosovo, and Macedonia, among other places.

After the Cold War in Western Europe, various factors would eventually decrease the urgency of most territorial minority and separatist issues. The demise of communism and the disappearance of the Soviet Union was a hefty political-ideological and financial drain for various separatist movements. In some countries, far-reaching political and constitutional changes were introduced. This type of change, which in countries like Spain was a by-product of democratization, can have an ambiguous effect on territorially based minority issues. Democracy and regionalism enjoy an ambivalent relationship. As indicated: democratization practically always gives minorities more cultural and political freedom and autonomy. This may stimulate or mitigate nationalist enthusiasm. Democratization may open up new possibilities for conflict resolution, such as the devolution of legislative and executive power that followed the death of Franco in 1975, in Spain. But democratic governments may also feel constrained by public opinion and political support to compromise in the struggle against allegedly subversive and terrorist organization, and in exceptional cases the need for democratic legitimacy and support may even incite governments to politicize the question and to seek confrontation rather than reconciliation. The administrative changes in United Kingdom during the 1990s created a new level of self-rule for its constituent parts. After a referendum in 1997, Scotland re-established its own parliament, for the first time since 1707, after the Acts of Union with the Kingdom of England. Around the same time, Wales proclaimed its first people's assembly in the history of the region. Electoral support for the Scottish National Party (SNP) had long remained limited, reaching its lowest point during the 1950s. SNP backing fluctuated considerably during the following decades, with a breakthrough during 1967–74, recurring setbacks in the 1980s and an initially hesitant but eventually convincing comeback from the 1990s into the 2000s. Scottish regionalism/nationalism culminated in 2014. In September, a referendum was held on the independence of Scotland: 1.6 million Scots voted for independence from the United Kingdom; slightly over 2 million voted against.

In Spain, the death of Generalissimo Franco (November 1975) marked the end of a strictly centralized, authoritarian Spanish state and the suppression of regional languages and cultures, including those of the Basque population. Under the new democratic government, the Basques acquired a considerable degree of autonomy, which they formally accepted through a referendum in 1979. However, the leaders of the ETA, founded in December 1958, and its political arm Herri Batasuna (Unity of the People, established in 1978) maintained the armed struggle for independence, which would continue until early 2011, when ETA announced a 'permanent' ceasefire. The armed struggle had cost hundreds of lives. Although the conflict in Northern Ireland is not a typical minority's issue, the armed struggle of the Irish Republican Army (IRA) showed many similarities with that of the ETA [170]. In the same way, the IRA officially terminated its armed struggle against the British occupying forces. In April 1998, an agreement was reached between the governments in London and Dublin and the major political parties in the northern part of Ireland. This Good Friday Agreement was agreed after extensive US mediation, and it provided, among other things, self-government for Northern Ireland, with the active participation of Sinn Féin, the political arm of the IRA. In 2005, the IRA announced an end to its armed struggle, which would eventually facilitate the formation of a government between the Protestant Democratic Unionist Party and its Catholic competitor and former arch-enemy Sinn Féin, in May 2007. Although Northern Ireland still struggles with the consequences of years of civil war and military intervention, the militant splits from the IRA that never accepted the peace agreement and IRA's demobilization seemed to have lost the sympathy and the support of larger segments of society. Since the early 1970s, when political violence in Northern Ireland erupted, more than 3,000 citizens and servicemen have died.

In the context of the minorities' question in Europe after the Cold War, it was especially the steady influx of new immigrants and the changing composition of the population which would come to dominate the political agenda. At the same time that Europeans were 'witnessing the breakdown of the "homogenous nation" ... and the emergence ... of looser poly-ethnic societies' [159: 117], the issues of national identity, long forgotten, neglected or avoided for reasons of political correctness, reappeared in the public debate. Few Europeans seemed to want to realize that they lived in immigration countries. Integration and assimilation became heavily charged concepts in post–Cold War Europe, laden with expectations and frustrations. In the larger public mind, integration is as much about complying with the host state's laws and other legal rules as it is about accepting and internalizing important cultural norms and values of the majority population. The concentration of migrants in the poorer districts of the larger cities and suburbs, the distinct language, culture and religion of many migrants, the congruence of ethnic diversity and disparities in education and income, the relatively high levels of unemployment, social security dependence, and crime among some minority groups, as well as the fear and the realization that the violence and fundamentalism in the Muslim world would be imported into the societies of Western Europe, gave the immigration issue an unprecedented social and political acuity. Together with European integration, the immigration issue generated a stronger emphasis on the political significance of the nation and national identity. They came to play a critical role in the revival of radical nationalism in European politics.

Concerns about the impact of immigration and ethnic diversity in post–Cold War Europe manifested themselves in many different ways, from critical interventions in the public and political debate to expressions of xenophobia and racist violence. Initially, violence against migrants in the reunited Germany attracted most attention. The incidents typically concerned non-European ethnic minorities, Asians and Africans, living in the former German Democratic Republic. The rapid and deep changes in Germany's Eastern *Länder*, the mood of uncertainty and insecurity among the population and the lack of a public democratic culture were at the basis of the disturbances. In September 1991, a daylong siege of a shelter for foreign refugees in Hoyerswerda led to the clearance and forced relocation of its inhabitants. In August a year later, another accommodation in a suburb of Rostock was evacuated, after it had been subject to an arson attack by local residents. The violence did not remain limited to foreigners or asylum seekers in the eastern part of Germany. An arson attack on an apartment building in Mölln, near Hamburg, in November 1992, cost the lives of three Turkish inhabitants. Half a year later, in May 1993, five Turkish women died in a fire in Solingen, in the Ruhr area. These actions were attributed to right-wing extremist groups, apparently incited by extreme nationalist and 'anti-foreigner' ideas. In other cases, especially also in the incidents in the eastern part of Germany, larger groups of troublemakers were involved.

Unlike from the German Democratic Republic, West Germany had always received particularly large number of immigrants. Three categories of émigrés could be distinguished: during the Cold War, guest workers or labour migrants came mostly from Turkey and the Western Balkans; after the Cold War, political refugees arrived from former Yugoslavia and other conflict zones; and throughout the post-war decades, individuals of German descent came in from Russia and other Eastern European countries. Approximately 13 million Germans from Central and Eastern Europe had fled to the Western part of the country between 1944 and 1947. By 1950, out of the 50.8 million people living in Western Germany, 7.9 million were refugees and expellees. Another 1.6 million Germans would flee the German Democratic Republic. By 1960, German refugees accounted for almost a quarter, 23.8 per cent, of the population of West Germany [131: 434]. In 1988, two years before reunification, Germany had an immigration surplus of 550,000 people. This would double during the next two years, around the time the above-mentioned incidents took place. In 1988, 103,000 persons asked for political asylum in Germany. The number grew to 121,000 in 1989 and to 193,000, 256,000 and 450,000 in 1990–2. Altogether, between 1991 and 2003, Germany reached a migration surplus of 14.6 million people.[4]

The rise of political nationalism in Europe is particularly significant for the advance of its 'ethnic' variant. The national question has again acquired a pronounced ethnic dimension. It is manifested in a drastically changed political discourse as well as in the proliferation of a range of new political parties and organizations with essentially nationalist agendas. The emergence of radical, mostly right-wing, nationalist parties and policies [2; 11; 126] is probably the most significant manifestation of post–Cold War nationalism in Europe. Nationalist parties have become a cross-European phenomenon. From the 1990s, they have not only enlarged popular support, but their ideas and beliefs have also entered mainstream political discourse in almost every European country. Not only have they become part of the 'normal electoral presence' [11: 9], but they have also become increasingly *salonfähig*, part of 'regular', 'acceptable' politics. Although relatively

---

[4] Figures come from different sources: see Jürgen Fijalkowski, 'Aggressive nationalism and immigration in Germany' [25: 142, 149, note 11]; Wasserstein [175: 763].

few nationalist parties have accepted governmental responsibility, in a growing number of countries they have entered more or less formal agreements to support coalition governments. The *cordon sanitaire* strategy against nationalist parties has become increasingly difficult to maintain. In most countries, it was not even tried anymore – nationalist parties have become too electorally big and too politically interesting to ignore. Paradoxically, few other containment approaches have proven to be more successful than saddling nationalist parties with actual governmental responsibility. In most cases where radical parties participated in government, their presence was short-lived and eventually ended in electoral defeat.

Right-wing radicalism in Germany has always attracted much attention, but it never established a significant presence factor in German national politics. Die Republikaner party, established in 1983, the more radical Deutsche Volksunion or German People's Union (1971) and the Nationaldemokratische Partei Deutschlands (National-Democratic Party of Germany) have from the early 1960s gained electoral successes at the regional level only, mainly in the eastern *Länder*. Political populism, which is a much larger political category than right-wing radicalism or extremism (the latter being practically 'marginal' by nature), has also generally remained of limited relevance in Germany. The closest to a populist party is Die Linke (The Left), the left-wing successor to the former ruling communist party in the German Democratic Republic. As yet, there has not been a Jörg Haider, Jean-Marie Le Pen, Pim Fortuyn or even Geert Wilders in Germany – that is to say, a radical populist politician who succeeded in gathering nationwide support and influence. But the public mood has certainly changed since the late 1990s. The economist Thilo Sarrazin apparently touched a raw nerve with his book *Deutschland schafft sich ab*, 'Germany Abolishes Itself', in which he discussed the nature and scope of immigration and the continuing reluctance among the (Turkish) minority to assimilate as major threats to the German welfare state [144]. It was the bestselling political book of the decade. By 2014, populism based on the same twin arguments of Euroscepticism and anti-immigration that are known from other European countries manifested itself in Germany too. The Eurosceptic Alternative für Deutschland (Alternative for Germany) secured parliamentary representation in various eastern provinces and in the European parliament. The PEGIDA movement, a German abbreviation for Patriotic Europeans against the Islamization of the West (Patriotische Europäer gegen die Islamisierung des Abendlandes), is also based in the eastern part of Germany, especially in Dresden, from where it organized weekly demonstrations against the rising tide of immigration in the country. Mainstream politicians responded ambivalently. Chancellor Angela Merkel criticized the anti-European and anti-Islamic positions of the Alternative party and the PEGIDA movement, although earlier Merkel herself had already openly admitted in October 2010, on the Germany Day of the young Christian Democrats, that the multicultural society had 'failed completely' – *absolut gescheitert*. Her audience agreed enthusiastically.

Merkel's critique of multiculturalism was illustrative of the extent to which the debate on immigration and integration had changed in Europe. It would have been unthinkable for any German political leader, and especially for a *Bundeskanzler*, to express the kind of ideas that had meanwhile become mainstream. In other countries, which were not hindered by the same historical baggage as Germany, similar changes occurred, only earlier and more drastic. *The* nationalist party in Europe is the Front National in France. Although the Front National has never carried any administrative responsibility at the national level and it has never had more than a marginal presence in the nation's legislature, the party has established itself as a permanent, albeit very controversial part of the French political landscape. Jean-Marie Le Pen, who founded the party in 1972 and who in 2011 handed leadership over to his daughter Marine, had his finest hour during the presidential vote of 2002. In the first round of the elections, he finished with 4.8 million votes (16.8 per cent), before the socialist candidate Lionel Jospin. In the second round, Le Pen lost against the incumbent President Jacques Chirac (1995–2007), reluctantly supported by the left part of the French electorate. In Italy, another country with long-time radically nationalist parties, the Alleanza Nationale (National Alliance), successor (1995) to the neo-fascist Movimento Sociale Italiano (Social Movement of Italy), was part of government coalitions led by Silvio Berlusconi and his Forza Italia during the 1990s and 2000s. By the time the party joined the coalition, it had already shifted to the political centre, under the leadership of the later Vice-Prime Minister and Minister of Foreign Affairs Gianfranco Fini. In February 2000, the Freedom Party of Austria (Freiheitliche Partei Österreichs, FPÖ) joined the cabinet of the Christian Democratic Prime Minister Wolfgang Schüssel. The party had gained a historic 26.9 per cent in the national elections of the year before. Governmental responsibility gained by the FPÖ triggered the other member states of the European Union to briefly isolate Austria – 'for legitimizing the extreme right'. Relations between Vienna and Brussels were temporarily kept at the lowest workable level. Two years later, the Freedom Party lost almost 17 per cent of its electoral support, but still returned to government. In April 2005, after much internal turmoil, party leader Jörg Haider and other prominent figures left the FPÖ and founded a new conservative party: the Alliance for the Future of Austria (Bündnis Zukunft Österreich, BZÖ). It would take the FPÖ another ten years of internal strife and conflict before it recovered from Haider's defection. As with other nationalist and populist parties, the FPÖ and BZÖ are ideologically eclectic, combining elements of conservatism, libertarianism and liberalism, with a clear focus on anti-immigration, anti-EU and anti-Islam.

The Vlaams Blok (Flemish Bloc; from the end of 2004, the Vlaams Belang, the Flemish Interest) has been active in Flemish politics from the late 1970s. The party platform combines Flemish nationalism (and separatism) with anti-immigration positions. Most other political parties in Flanders have consistently and effectively boycotted the Flemish Interest through a *cordon sanitaire* strategy. The party took 24.2 per cent of the popular vote in the elections for the Flemish parliament in 2004 – its best result ever. In later elections, the party repeatedly lost support, due to more competition on the nationalist right, especially from the New Flemish Alliance (Nieuw-Vlaamse Alliantie or N-VA), established in 2001. From the mid-2000s, the N-VA became the most popular representative of the Flemish case, eventually becoming the largest party in the Flemish and national parliaments. The N-VA is not less insistent on the particular interests of Flanders, but it discards the strong anti-immigrant or anti-Muslim sentiments of the Flemish Interest. Having never been ostracized by Belgium's traditional political parties, the N-VA governed Flanders and was active at the federal level too. Different from most other nationalist parties, including Flemish Interest, the N-VA is pronouncedly pro-European, a sentiment it shares with some other regionalist parties, such as the Scottish National Party, but not with all.

The situation of the radical right in the former communist part of Europe is mixed. Some of the most significant nationalist parties have manifested themselves in the eastern part of Europe, particularly in the Balkans. The Croatian Democratic Union (Hrvatska Demokratska Zajednica or HDZ) was founded in June 1989 and would become Franjo Tudman's vehicle to presidential power. President and party took on a radically nationalist profile and were both responsible for the war crimes committed during the Yugoslav Civil War, especially in Bosnia and in the eastern part of Croatia. The HDZ remained the most powerful party in Croatia throughout the 1990s. After the death of Tudman in 1999, the party went through an ideological and electoral crisis, from which it has since remarkably recovered. Under new leadership and with a more moderate outlook, the party spent another eight years in government, from 2003 to 2011. Popular support for the HDZ gradually decreased from more than 40 per cent during the 1990s to 30 per cent in the 2000s and slightly over 20 per cent during the general elections in 2011. The Socijalistička Partija Srbije (Socialist Party of Serbia) of Slobodan Milošević was a similarly radical nationalist party, which dominated Serbian politics during the first decade after the collapse of Yugoslavia. The Socialist Party was alternately in open conflict and in cooperation with the even more blatantly nationalist Srpska Radikalna Stranka (Serbian Radical Party), founded by Vojislav Šešelj. Eventually, Šešelj would join Milošević at the International Criminal Tribunal for the Former Yugoslavia (ICTY) in The Hague, together with Radovan Karadžić, leader of the equally nationalistic Srpska Demokratska Stranka, the Serb Democratic Party in Bosnia and Herzegovina.

In most of the other countries in East-Central Europe, the appeal of radically nationalist parties remained limited throughout the 1990s. This was remarkable, given the social consequences of the deep political and economic reforms the post-communist countries implemented. Paradoxically, political nationalism would rise again from the early 2000s, after accession to the European Union. During the first post-communist decade, in most countries in East-Central Europe, the political elites shared a common agenda of political and economic transformation, including democratization and the building of a market economy. Radical nationalism may not have been absent, but it remained marginal or under the surface. The requirements for accession into the European Union left little room for political radicalism. It produced a shift to the political centre. In this respect, actual membership of the Union returned 'normal' politics to the post-communist countries of East-Central Europe. Accession into the EU paved the way again for political divergence, including political nationalism. Radically nationalist parties in East-Central Europe would recruit their popular support at least partially based on their anti-European ideas and ambitions. The role, relevance and outlook of radically nationalist parties can differ per country, but they are not without clear commonalities. Vigorously nationalist political parties in Europe are a mixed bag, closely resembling the deeply Eurosceptical and anti-European parties discussed before, insofar as nationalist and Eurosceptical parties do not overlap. Nationalism is a changeable and heterogeneous phenomenon, and so are the parties that either claim to be principally nationalist or that are labelled so by others. In line with the earlier definition, a radically nationalist political party is a party or movement that takes the 'nation' as the ultimate source, core and context of its political identity and action. Typically of nationalism, the left-right distinction is not particularly relevant. Nationalist groups in contemporary Europe are generally situated on the right of the political spectrum, but there are important exceptions. Especially in East-Central Europe, (former) communist parties combine fierce nationalism with leftist, often Marxist ideas. In Western Europe too, political parties sometimes combine nationalist ideas with leftist socio-economic ambitions. A more important distinction among nationalist parties is between the regionalist and separatist parties that promote a sub-national identity, on the one hand, and parties that aim to strengthen the national state and identity, on the other. It is especially the latter type of nationalist political parties, those with a national agenda, that have become relevant in post–Cold War Europe. Most of the parties that were mentioned earlier belong to this category, including the Front National in France, the Austrian FPÖ, and Geert Wilders' Party for Freedom in the Netherlands. Some nationalist parties have their membership base in specific ethnic groups, especially in East-Central Europe, but most parties clearly aim to represent the majority population, allegedly ignored by established parties. Another helpful though fleeting distinction is between nationalist parties and 'extremist' nationalist parties. Extremely nationalist, loud, aggressive and sometimes violent parties have remained a fringe phenomenon in practically all European countries, limited in popular support and electoral success. The parties that were discussed in these pages are clearly nationalist, in some respects even radically nationalist, but they are not extremist or violent. Racism is not a particularly conspicuous feature among the nationalist parties in Europe. Jean-Marie Le Pen, long-time leader of the Front National, occasionally used racist language and biological metaphors to phrase his political ideas. It was one of the major reasons why he was sidelined in his own party. Generally, anti-immigrant ideas and rhetoric are mostly couched in a combination of national political and cultural references, not racist ones.

Nationalist parties thrive on feelings of fear and insecurity, generated by rapid and fundamental societal changes. They mobilize support mainly on the basis of a negative agenda and tend to be distrustful and oppositional [11]. Practically every nationalist party shares a strong antipathy towards the EU and immigration, especially of non-Europeans. They share the conviction that 'Islamization' is a clear and present danger in most of their countries, for their national polities, their cultures and identities.

Nationalist parties are often identified with populist ones. Political nationalism and populism overlap, but they are not identical. The essential distinction is in the realm of ideas. Populism as an ideology is chameleonic; it lacks core values [166: 5]. Political nationalism may also be elastic, but it certainly has a key value, the self-defined interest of the nation and the national state. But they have much in common too. As populist political parties generally do, nationalist parties stand for personalized politics. They are political movements rather than parties. They are strongly leadership focused, not organization based. Charismatic political individuals dominate most nationalist parties. Geert Wilders' Party for Freedom has no membership, apart from Wilders himself. Nationalists and populists share 'a fundamental ambivalence about politics', as Taggart [166: 3] phrases it, and about representative democratic politics in particular. They operate within the boundaries of a representative democratic system, which they however fiercely critique. Nationalists and populists especially discard the institutions of indirect and representative democracy, including the traditional political parties and occasionally parliament. They suggest an ever wider gap between the 'people', virtuous and inherently good, and the political 'elite', indifferent and fundamentally alienated from the common men [2: 3]. The 'Euro' elite in Brussels is of course the superlative exemplar of a parasitical political elite.

Populists and nationalists pretend to give a voice to those citizens, particularly of the ethnic majority, who feel threatened by societal changes and who no longer feel represented in the existing political order. The final chapter will further elaborate and draw conclusions on the linkage between these three crucial notions of post-war history: nationalism, democracy and European integration. How will they develop, individually and in their mutual relationship?

4 Nationalism, Democracy and European Integration

The rapid turnover of grand ideas on global politics is indicative of the complexity, the volatility and the uncertainty of the world after the Cold War. Seemingly paradigmatic notions such as the end of history [47], the clash of civilizations [78] or the unipolar moment [101] have come and gone. In Europe, few other ideas were as widely discussed academically as the crisis of the nation state. The power and autonomy of the national state were to be gradually undermined from below, by ever more culturally diverse and assertive societies, and from above, through the simultaneous processes of globalization and European integration. Meanwhile, however, the national state has reasserted itself impressively. The 'return' of the nation state in crucial parts of the world is visible through the re-emergence of the norms of national sovereignty and non-intervention in global politics, Russia and China being its prime protagonists. The reaffirmation of the national state, its protective and regulatory roles, was further promoted by such diverse global phenomena as the emergence of Islamic terrorism and the global financial crisis. In Europe, the Eurozone crisis in combination with other transnational developments, especially immigration, weakened popular support for European integration and strengthened the focus on the national state. So while overall the power and efficacy of the national state in Europe may have weakened, its status and legitimacy seem to have increased considerably. The essence of the shifting of politics away from the national state was not that the state lost significance across the board, but that it became less significant in some areas but not in others. This created specific challenges. Particularly, the growing discrepancy between the declining functionality of the state in socio-economic and financial matters and the unwavering, if not increased, appreciation of the national state as an object of political identity and loyalty proved problematic.

It is extremely difficult to establish the weight of nationalism among the many factors that have defined political change in Europe during and after the Cold War. It is even often problematic to assess whether nationalism is a cause or a consequence of important events and developments. This book is based on the assumption that political nationalism, that is, political action plausibly guided by a distinct idea of the nation or a strong sense of national identity, played an important role in key developments such as the collapse of communism, the disintegration of multinational states and the establishment of new ones. This also applies to other changes that were discussed in this book, including the development of the welfare state, the rise of Euroscepticism, the critique of multiculturalism and the emergence of nationalist political parties. Nationalist thought has gained considerable significance in Europe after the Cold War, and there is not much reason to believe that it will fade anytime soon. Two decades into the post–Cold War era, the continuing role and relevance of national identities and nationalism are broadly acknowledged. Much has changed since Breuilly argued, in the early 1980s, that the days of nationalism have 'largely passed'. Scholars of such different views as Hobsbawm and Francis Fukuyama agreed on the fact that at the end of the twentieth century, nationalism had lost much of its historic import. '[T]he final political neutralization of nationalism may not occur in this generation or the next', Fukuyama opined, but that 'does not affect the prospect of its ultimately taking place' [47: 275]. Fukuyama's expectation came very close to Hobsbawm's observation that nationalism had passed its peak. Historians have routinely emphasized the transient nature of nationalism, but every so often they had to come to the conclusion that nationalism had proved less ephemeral that they had expected or hoped for. This final chapter will summarize the main findings and conclusions regarding the history of nationalism in post-war Europe, and it will reflect on the vitally important link between nationalism, democracy and integration across the continent.

In the concluding pages of *Nations and Nationalism in a Global Era*, Antony Smith [157] discusses the main arguments for and against nationalism. On an intellectual level, nationalism seems illogical and its major assumptions flawed, Smith argues. The world was never neatly divided into specific nations or nation states, each with its own apparently unique past, present and future. The nation has never been and will probably never be the source of all political loyalty, legitimacy or power. Individuals do not necessarily identify with the nation, or with the nation only. On the other hand, nations and nationalism have proven remarkably persistent. As Smith asserts: 'As long as any global order is based on a balance of competing states, so long will the principle of nationality provide the only widely acceptable legitimation of focus of popular mobilization' [157: 154]. The ethical or moral argument *against* nationalism emphasizes that nationalism is radical, if not extremist and divisive. Nationalism would deny individual freedom and diversity. It divides people; it leads to conflict. The post-war history of Europe, especially after the Cold War, gave ample evidence of the corrupting and divisive nature of nationalism, in both Eastern and Western Europe. But recent history has also shown the other, positive and constructive features of nationalism. Persistently strong national identities sustained peoples' legitimate ambitions for freedom and independence and also supported the largely peaceful formation of new, sometimes resurgent national states, especially in East-Central Europe and in the former Soviet Union. Finally, not all 'nationalisms' are automatically radical or extremist, and nationalist thought can be combined with multiple forms of politics, including democratic ones. Nationalism exercises a strongly unifying force, which can arguably be seen as a condition for the solidarity that sustains modern democracies and welfare states. The geopolitical argument against nationalism is equally contentious. Nationalism, whether deeply ingrained or politically constructed, played an important, motivating role in many of the late or post-communist 'new' wars and other conflicts [90] that were discussed in this book. These tribulations cost the lives of many thousands of Europeans. Nationalist conflicts and wars have also had a strongly destabilizing effect on international peace and security. However, the very same peace and stability of our international order is also built on the sovereignty, diversity and unique identity of nations and states, not infrequently perceived as a *national* identity. Nationalism underpins the distinctiveness of individual states and the plurality of the international state system.

In the contemporary usage of the word 'nationality', it often refers to the primarily political and legal concept of citizenship.

One's nationality is one's citizenship, as evidenced by one's passport. But nationality or citizenship are more than just legal concepts. They reflect an often deep cultural and psychological feeling of belonging, being a member of the national community, sharing a common national identity. For many people, national identity continues to provide the 'good' that other forms of identity apparently fail to do, or fail to do to the same extent. But the focus of national identity is not necessarily the country where one resides. In today's world, globalization, migration and integration have loosened the link between nationality or citizenship and national identity. Individuals may leave their homeland to live and work in another country, while remaining in constant contact with, and continuing to feel deep or primary loyalty to, their place of origin. One of the most prolific authors on the political consequences of worldwide digitalization suggests that such different aspects of globalization as easily accessible and shareable information and cheap transportation have actually strengthened rather than weakened nationalism. 'Nationalism ... is going through a major revival on the Web', Evgeni Morozov writes. 'Perhaps, nationalism and the Internet are something of natural allies' [125: 248–9]. Displaced people meet on the Internet, and diaspora communities remain in contact with each other and with the motherland online. Every type of information about any national issue or conflict is easily available, including extremist, xenophobic and other material that would otherwise have remained out of sight, or that would not have been published at all. In conclusion, there is no reason to expect that nationalism or national identity will be weakened or undermined by the revolutionary acceleration of worldwide communication or information that we have witnessed from the late twentieth century. Rather, the opposite is the case.

Smith summarizes the underlying functions of national identity and nationalism as basic answers to the ephemerality, the oblivion and the loneliness of the individual. National identity links the individual with the longer and wider framework of the nation, thereby offering him or her a sense of community, dignity and fraternity [156: 160–2]. While travelling through the troubled lands of Eastern Europe during the early 1990s, the essayist and politician Michael Ignatieff learned exactly the same. 'It is not enough to be a people', he concluded. 'In order to have respect, you must have a nation' [80: 102]. Paradoxically perhaps, nationhood and citizenship seem to have become more rather than less important in post-war Europe. They are critical not only for reasons of identity and belonging, but also for less prosaic purposes such as the provision of physical safety or welfare benefits. The building of the welfare state was one of the most important *national* developments in Europe after the Second World War.

Still, the political relevance of nationalism has fluctuated sharply during the post-war decades, both in Western and in Eastern Europe. These fluctuations were partly determined by developments from beyond the continent. The second half of the twentieth century was a time of great turbulence and change. Some of these changes have stalled and have been reversed, but others have proved permanent. This book was structured around three such developments: the occupation and the division of the continent by the United States and the Soviet Union, in a sense outside powers; the process of cooperation and integration in Western Europe and the communist experiment in Eastern Europe; and the more recent effects of migration and societal and (geo)political change in Europe after the Cold War.

No other development had a greater impact on the significance of nationalism into the nation than the process of European integration. Beginning initially in the Western part, and later also spreading in Southern and Eastern Europe, integration resulted from a complex combination of geopolitical conditions, realist concerns and idealist ambitions, of which among the most deeply felt was the determination to effectively deal with Europe's history of nationalist conflict and war. If the process of European integration is evaluated and put in a longer historical perspective, the conclusions are mixed. The specific and unique combination of international cooperation and supranational integration in the context of the European Union has largely eliminated the destructive power of nationalism among its member states. Nationalism as a cause of armed conflict or war between member states of the Union is unlikely. European integration also, albeit to a lesser extent, contributed to the weakening of the destructive force of nationalism within states – nationalism as a motivation for political repression, for dictatorship, but also for inter-ethnic conflict. Interestingly, however, European integration has also raised its own variant of nationalist thought, namely radical Euroscepticism or anti-Europeanism.

European integration has fundamentally changed the continent. Until fairly recently, most observers would have added that it transformed Europe irreversibly. That confidence has since been shaken. After the Cold War, 'Europe' has widened and it has deepened, but European integration also seems to have lost part of its certainty. The lore and the lure of 'ever-closer union' has much been tarnished. During the Eurozone crisis, for the first time in the history of European integration, the exit of member states was openly and widely discussed (also beyond the radically Eurosceptical parties) as a serious, perhaps even a necessary, option. Discussions were held in member states considering leaving the EU, especially the United Kingdom, and in others who deliberated over the exit of problematic members, especially Greece. For the first time in the history of European integration, the Lisbon Treaty contained a formal provision for members who wish to leave the Union, Article 49A.2.

Different from the process of European integration, the dismantling of the great European colonial empires unquestionably belonged to the permanent changes after the Second World War. It took less than a generation to reduce Europe's great colonial powers to mainstream national states. Only the Soviet Union survived as an imperial power. But Russia has always been an empire and a national state combined. Geographically, administratively and for many citizens of Russia also emotionally, there was no clear division or distinction between Russia and its 'colonies'. When the Soviet Union ceased to exist, the Russian people not only lost their empire; they also lost their national 'state' as they knew it. In every respect, the collapse of the Soviet Union was one of the landmark moments in the history of the late twentieth century. It put an end to the geopolitical division of Europe and to the Cold War between East and West. It radically altered regional and global power relations. Eventually, it would also inspire a revisionist foreign policy, once the Russian leadership had put its own house in order and attempted to regain some of its earlier international clout.

As difficult as it is to isolate nationalism from other aspects which figured in the complex history of communist collapse and state disintegration, it seems safe to assume that nationalism has not been the only or the decisive factor. A range of longer-term political and economic developments gradually undermined the communist order. These weakened the purposiveness of the communist rulers and the legitimacy of their political order so dramatically that the regimes would essentially implode. Very few people were ultimately willing and able to defend communism. For an empire, the Soviet Union collapsed unprecedentedly peacefully. Nationalist ambitions triggered armed conflicts in different parts of the (former) Soviet Union, but they also contributed to the largely non-violent dismantling of the communist 'bloc'. The disintegration of the *Pax Sovietica* was the final chapter in the exciting history of the relationship between communism and nationalism in Europe. Communism coloured nationalism. Nationalism shaped communism, including its demise. Western Europe underwent substantially different but equally fundamental developments after the Second World War. The changes in this part of the continent unfolded more gradually and consensually, but they also proved significantly more durable. Compared to the interwar years, democracy in Western Europe became essentially uncontested. Despite challenges to the form and substance of democracy, a distinction which allows for such different political events as de Gaulle's elimination of the French Fourth Republic and the terrorist acts of Baader-Meinhof or the Red Brigades, it survived intact. Thus far, the democratic order proved flexible enough to combine with all major political and socio-economic changes in post-war European history: integration, the welfare state, globalization, immigration and the increasing diversity of population. Western Europe was also deeply impacted by the end of the Cold War. In a sense, Western Europe ceased to exist after 1989; it was no longer a separate geographical and geopolitical entity – and neither was Eastern Europe.

Political nationalism came with ups and downs in post-war Europe, but after the Cold War its political urgency increased, across the continent. In Eastern Europe, nationalism worked as an antidote against communist ideology and the Soviet-dominated (inter)national order, and it was at the basis of state collapse and state formation, in conjunction with other political ideas and ambitions. In many Western European countries, a resurgent political nationalism was mostly aimed against the perceived threats to the nation and the nation state, and against the alleged violations of national sovereignty and identity by the often-anonymous forces of globalization and European integration and the more immediate consequences of immigration. There is little reason to expect that nationalism will fade into obscurity anytime soon. '[N]ationalism continues to be used as the basic organizing principle for

135

both democratic and non-democratic states worldwide', concludes Claire Sutherland, 'providing further evidence of the ideology's enduring power, flexibility and diversity in the twenty-first century' [164: 102]. Post–Cold War Europe not only witnessed the re-emergence of nationalism but also the adjustment of democracy. Democracy is a crucial aspect of any claim, by any regime type, to political legitimacy. The liberal concept of democracy, though ideologically dominant in the early post–Cold War years, has meanwhile been stripped of its alleged universalism. Scholars and politicians have equipped democracy with a series of adjectives, all meant to qualify its allegedly universal liberal nature. 'Illiberal', 'electoral' and 'guided' democracy were among the early scholarly qualifications [40]. 'Russian' democracy or democracy with 'Chinese characters' were later added by the political elites in these countries to emphasize the typically national nature of their democratic variant and to distinguish it from the still-dominant 'Western' interpretation. Arguably, the legitimacy of authoritarian regimes rests not only on 'performance' (prosperity, stability and security) but also on shared values, including manipulative but powerful notions such as national identity and national interest. But also in countries where the liberal democratic order remained essentially undisputed, as in practically all of the member states of the European Union, the actual functioning and the future adaptability of representative democracy were increasingly questioned. One aspect of the rethinking of democracy that is particularly important for the purpose of this book, is the question of how democracy will continue to relate to national identity and to nationalism. Can political democracy be solely based on individual or political rights, or does it need a collective cultural or ethnic awareness too? Does a civic concept of the nation suffice for a sustainable democratic state and society? Can democracy also develop beyond the boundaries of the nation state, in the larger European 'space'?

Nationalism and (modern) democracy are historically related phenomena. They developed simultaneously, in mutual connection and as part of the same comprehensive historical process of modernization. 'Democracy was born with the sense of nationality', as the American historian Liah Greenfeld [61: 10] puts it. Greenfeld acknowledges that nationalism, especially in its civic and moderate expression, contributed positively to the development of democracy, if only because democracy was almost exclusively shaped within the context of the national state. Scholarship has often highlighted the divisive and confrontational nature of nationalist politics, and emphasized the subversive impact that nationalism has historically had on democracy. The counter-argument, which says that nationalism positively impacts on democracy, has a long pedigree too. It goes back to eighteenth- and nineteenth-century liberal thinkers such as J.-J. Rousseau and J. S. Mill. But also in the current debate some scholars emphasize that nationalism is actually a precondition for liberal democracy [120; 167; 185]. Others [112; 161] have focused on a more disturbing aspect of the democracy-nationalism nexus, stressing the argument that premature democratization easily provokes nationalism and nationalist conflict.

There is a temporal and a spatial dimension to the relationship between nationalism and democracy. Without denying their earlier historical roots, both emerged in the late eighteenth century, in Western Europe. The spread of nationalism can be linked with the rise of mass politics, and with growing popular political participation, which is also a vital condition of democracy (not a guarantee of course). Nationalism and democracy are principally egalitarian ideas. Everybody enjoys identical status as a member of the national and the political community. The people are equal and the people are sovereign. These are the foundations of nationalism and of democracy, at least in theory and principle, although not always in practice. For most of its earlier history, modern democracy remained limited to specific segments of society, defined by material standards, gender and in some countries also race. Nationalism almost by definition considered only members of its 'own' nation as equal. From Europe and the United States, nationalism and democracy spread to all four corners of the world, although nationalism more rapidly, widely and deeply than democracy. The mutual relationship between nationalism and democracy has indeed remained complex, and often conflictual. In Europe, nationalism was a major and occasionally effective instrument of anti-democratic mobilization during the first half of the twentieth century. Liberal democracy and the welfare state did much to mitigate the attractiveness of radical political nationalism afterwards.

There is also an important spatial aspect that nationalism and democracy share, namely that specifically modern form of territorial-political organization known as the national or occasionally as the nation state. Nationalism moved the primary basis of political loyalty and legitimacy away from the king, emperor or empire to the nation and the national state. Nationalism is the political doctrine, the political idea that not only aims at the independent, sovereign national state where it is absent, but also ideationally underpins the state where it is present. In this respect, nationalism, or national identity, works as a condition for democracy. Democracy developed within the geographical, political and emotional confines of the national state. Arguably, no viable state, or democracy, flourishes without a developed sense of national identity. A firm, tolerant and peaceful sense of nationality reinforces the feelings of solidarity and belonging which support the modern (welfare) state to function properly inwardly and towards the outside world.

These observations are all based on past experience. They do not necessarily reveal much about the future dynamics between democracy, nationalism and the national state. How will nationalism and democracy impact each other in the foreseeable future?

There is ample argument that nationalism will continue to contribute to the strength and vitality of democracy. 'Nationalism is the cultural sensibility of sovereignty', Anthony Giddens says; '[it is] the concomitant of the co-ordination of administrative power within the bounded nation-state' [54: 219]. The argument is that national identity contributes to feelings of equality and unity, to civil commitment, to social obligations and to solidarity, all of which sustain a democratic polity. As a political body, democracy needs a sense of community to bring or keep together what is politically, economically, religiously or otherwise divided. The state is the source of legitimacy, but society is the source of unity, as the British philosopher Roger Scruton [149: 55] expressed it.

For most people, the commitment they feel towards their fellow nationals is different, more profound and extensive than they may have towards 'strangers', towards nationals from other countries. But even in those cases where these commitments may be weak or even absent, the contemporary welfare state has institutionalized them. In many ways, especially also financially, our modern democracy asks more from many of its citizens than any other political system, and it is questionable whether it would be able to do so effectively without it being rooted in a commonly shared identification with the nation and the state. Distributive justice of the extent of the current welfare state in Europe needs firm social support, and this requires the organized trust and solidarity that especially the national state and community bring. Of course, there is more to the welfare state than this normative or solidarity argument only. Rational considerations may also underpin it. Research indicates that the redistributive aspect of the welfare state makes the whole of society happier, rich and poor alike [177]. A fairer, more equal, stable and peaceful society benefits all citizens.

The flip side of this argument is equally relevant: the greater the internal diversity of society, including ethnic diversity, the more difficult it may be to keep these feelings of solidarity, and to normatively sustain the welfare state. Theoretically at least, the observation makes sense that the others with whom we share the 'fruits and the burdens' of our welfare arrangement must remain 'identifiable and familiar' [167: 118]. This goes for the national community and *mutatis mutandis* for organized solidarity at the European level too. Where diversity grows, trust and solidarity may require more effort. The European Union is a good case in point.

Democracy as we know it developed within the context of the national state. The concurrence between the territorially based form and the democratic content of politics has not changed significantly in post-war Europe. For the vast majority of Europeans, the national state is still the main source of political identity and legitimacy.

Finally, nationalism has a positive impact on the pluralist nature of the global political order. The nation state, when backed up by an assertive national identity or nationalism, preserves global diversity, including political liberalism. Various scholars have emphasized the positive contribution of nationalism to global diversity, from the perspective of either nationalism research [48] or International Relations [79].

Nationalism, or, more dispassionately, national identity, will probably continue to impact democracy. But will democracy also continue to affect nationalism? The easiest answer would be that political democracy is the most effective antidote against radical nationalism. No single developed democracy has ever engaged in radical, violent and aggressive forms of state nationalism either against its own citizens or against other states, as practically every ideological variant of authoritarianism has done. But the link between democracy and nationalism is problematic. The relationship between democratization and nationalist conflict in the context of post-communist politics in Eastern Europe was extensively discussed, and so was the more fundamental critique of nationalism as the politicization of ethnicity, to which no political regime is by definition immune. Nationalism as the 'the dark side of democracy' remains an important reminder of the potentially dangerous dimensions of democracy.

The relationship between the national state and the European Union has also grown increasingly challenging. The Eurozone crisis had a double, and potentially subversive, impact on the future of European integration. Further steps were taken to deepen the integration process, including the formation of a Banking Union, but at the very same time Euroscepticism reached new heights as well. After the mid-2014 elections, the European Parliament gathered more openly Eurosceptical and anti-European representatives than ever before. European integration continued to deepen, and Euroscepticism continued to rise. The relationship between European integration and the national state remains complex and diverse. There is little reason to argue that the process of European integration seriously weakened the national state. On the contrary, the national state enabled, sustained and restricted European integration. And the European Union *needs* strong member states. As Milward [122: 3] put it: 'To supersede the nation-state would be to destroy the community.' It still seems unlikely that the European Union will ever take over the normative and emotional functions of the nation state. If for many Europeans their attitude to the national state is determined by obligation ('my country, right or wrong'), their position towards the European Union is mostly defined by reason.

The twentieth century was the century of the Great European Civil War, of radical nationalism, of war and the collapse of colonial empires, of foreign domination, division and marginalization and eventually of Europe's unification again. However, the twentieth century was also the century of Europe's dynamism, its diversity, freedom and prosperity and, most of all, its admirable ability to change and adapt. Europe reinvents itself permanently: from the great European empires to the nation state, to the European Union.

Bibliography

[1] D. Albertazzi, 'Switzerland: Yet Another Populist Paradise', in D. Albertazzi and D. McDonnell (eds), *Twenty-First Century Populism: The Spectre of Western European Democracy* (Basingstoke: Palgrave Macmillan, 2008).

[2] D. Albertazzi and D. McDonnell, 'Introduction: The Sceptre and the Spectre', in D. Albertazzi and D. McDonnell (eds), *Twenty-First Century Populism: The Spectre of Western European Democracy* (Basingstoke: Palgrave Macmillan, 2008).

[3] D. Albertazzi and D. McDonnell (eds), *Twenty-First Century Populism: The Spectre of Western European Democracy* (Basingstoke: Palgrave Macmillan, 2008).

[4] B. Anderson, *Imagined Communities: Reflections on the Origin and Spread of Nationalism*, rev. ed. (London: Verso, 1993).

[5] B. Anderson, *The Spectre of Comparisons: Nationalism, Southeast Asia, and the World* (London–New York: Verso, 1998).

[6] M. Anderson *States and Nationalism in Europe since 1945* (London–New York: Routledge, 2000).

[7] R. Aron, *Progress and Disillusion: The Dialectics of Modern Society* (New York: Frederick A. Praeger, 1968).

[8] R. Augstein et al., *Historikerstreit. Die Dokumentation der Kontroverse um die Einzigartigkeit der nationalsozialistischen Judenvernichtung* (München–Zurich: Piper-Verlag, 1987).

[9] M. Beissinger, 'Nationalisms That Bark and Nationalisms That Bite: Ernest Gellner and the Substantiation of Nations', in J. A. Hall (ed.), *The State of the Nation: Ernest Gellner and the Theory of Nationalism* (Cambridge: Cambridge University Press, 1998).

[10] D. Bell, *The End of Ideology: On the Exhaustion of Political Ideas in the Fifties*, new rev. ed. (New York: Collier Books, 1961).

[11] M. Berezin, *Illiberal Politics in Neoliberal Times: Culture, Security and Populism in the New Europe* (New York: Cambridge University Press, 2009).

[12] R. A. Berman, *Anti-Americanism in Europe: A Cultural Problem* (Stanford, CA: Stanford University Press, 2004).

[13] M. Billig, *Banal Nationalism* (London: Sage Publications, 1995).

[14] Th. Borstelmann, *The 1970s: A New Global History from Civil Rights to Economic Inequality* (Princeton, NJ: Princeton University Press, 2012).

[15] K.-D. Bracher, *Zeit der Ideologien. Eine Geschichte politischen Denkens im 20. Jahrhundert* (Stuttgart: Deutsche Verlags-Anstalt, 1982).

[16] J. Breuilly, *Nationalism and the State* (Manchester: Manchester University Press, 1982).

[17] J. Breuilly, *Nationalism and the State*, 2nd ed. (Manchester: Manchester University Press, 1993).

[18] W. Brierley and L. Giacometti, 'Italian National Identity and the Failure of Regionalism', in B. Jenkins and S. A. Spyros (eds), *Nation & Identity in Contemporary Europe* (London–New York: Routledge, 1996).

[19] R. Brubaker, *Citizenship and Nationhood in France and Germany* (Cambridge, MA: Harvard University Press, 1992).

[20] R. Brubaker, *Nationhood Reframed–Nationhood and the National Question in the New Europe* (Cambridge: Cambridge University Press, 1996).

[21] R. Brubaker, 'The Manichean Myth: Rethinking the Distinction between "Civic" and "Ethnic" Nationalism', in H. Kriesi et al. (eds), *Nation and National Identity: The European Experience in Perspective* (Zürich: Verlag Rüegger, 1999).

[22] Y. M. Brudny, *Reinventing Russia: Russian Nationalism and the Soviet State, 1953–1991* (Cambridge, MA: Harvard University Press, 1998).

[23] Z. K. Brzezinski, *The Soviet Bloc: Unity and Conflict* (Cambridge, MA: Harvard University Press, 1967).

[24] C. Calhoun, *Nations Matter: Culture, History, and the Cosmopolitan Dream* (Abingdon: Routledge, 2007).

[25] R. Caplan and J. Feffer (eds), *Europe's New Nationalism: States and Minorities in Conflict* (Oxford: Oxford University Press, 1996).

[26] E. H. Carr, *Nationalism and After* (London: Macmillan, 1945).

[27] E. H. Carr, *A History of Soviet Russia,* 14 volumes (London: Macmillan, 1950–69).

[28] H. Carrère d'Encausse, *L'Empire éclaté : La révolte des nations en U.R.S.S.* (Paris: Flammarion, 1978).

[29] W. Churchill, 'Speech to the Academic Youth 1946 – Zürich' (http://www.europa-web.de/europa/02wwswww/202histo/churchil.htm, 1946).

[30] St. Clissold (ed.), *Yugoslavia and the Soviet Union: A Documentary Survey* (Oxford: Oxford University Press, 1975).

[31] W. Connor, *Ethnonationalism: The Quest for Understanding* (Princeton, NJ: Princeton University Press, 1994).

[32] M. Conway, 'The Rise and Fall of Western Europe's Democratic Age 1945–73', *Contemporary European History*, vol. XIII (2004), pp. 67–88.

[33] M. van Creveld, *The Rise and Decline of the State* (Cambridge: Cambridge University Press, 1999).

[34] L. Crump, *The Warsaw Pact Reconsidered: International Relations in Eastern Europe, 1955–1969* (London: Routledge, 2015).

Bibliography

[35] *Dangers, Tests and Miracles: The Remarkable Life Story of Chief Rabbi Rosen of Romania as Told to Joseph Finklestone* (London: Weidenfeld & Nicolson, 1990).

[36] G. Delanty and K. Kumar (eds), *The Sage Handbook of Nations and Nationalism* (London: Sage Publications, 2006).

[37] K. W. Deutsch, *Nationalism and Its Alternatives* (New York: Alfred A. Knopf, 1969).

[38] I. Deutscher, *Stalin: A Political Biography* (Oxford: Oxford University Press, 1949).

[39] D. R. Devereux, 'The End of Empires: Decolonization and Its Repercussions', in K. Larres (ed.), *A Companion to Europe since 1945* (Oxford: Wiley Blackwell, 2013).

[40] L. Diamond, 'Elections without Democracy: Thinking about Hybrid Regimes', *Journal of Democracy*, vol. 13, no. 2 (2002), pp. 21–35.

[41] A. Dieckhoff and C. Jaffrelot (eds), *Repenser le nationalisme. Théories et pratiques* (Paris: Presses de Sciences Po, 2006).

[42] F. Duchêne, 'Europe's Role in World Peace', in R. Mayne (ed.), *Europe Tomorrow* (London: Fontana, 1972).

[43] F. Duchêne, *Jean Monnet: The First Statesman of Interdependence* (New York–London: W.W. Norton & Company, 1994).

[44] G. Esping-Andersen, *The Three Worlds of Welfare Capitalism* (Cambridge: Polity Press, 2004).

[45] M. Freeden, 'Is Nationalism a Distinct Ideology?', *Political Studies*, vol. 46, no. 4 (1998), pp. 748–65.

[46] G. L. Freeze, *Russia: A History*, 3rd ed. (New York: Oxford University Press, 2009).

[47] F. Fukuyama, *The End of History and the Last Man* (London: Hamish Hamilton, 1992).

[48] E. Gellner, *Thought and Change* (London: Weidenfeld & Nicolson, 1964).

[49] E. Gellner, *Nations and Nationalism* (Oxford: Basil Blackwell, 1983).

[50] E. Gellner, *Conditions of Liberty: Civil Society and Its Rivals* (New York: Viking, 1994).

[51] A. W. M. Gerrits, *The Myth of Jewish Communism: A Historical Interpretation* (Frankfurt am Main: Peter Lang, 2009).

[52] A. W. M. Gerrits, 'Nationalisme en internationalisme in Europa na 1945', in L. H. M. Wessels and T. Bosch (eds), *Nationalisme, naties en staten. Europa vanaf circa 1800 tot heden* (Nijmegen: Van Tilt, 2012).

[53] A. W. M. Gerrits, 'Solidarity and the European Union: From the Welfare State to the Euro Crisis', in E. Hillebrand and A. M. Kellner (eds), *Shaping a Different Europe: Contributions to a Critical Debate* (Bonn: Dietz Verlag, 2015).

[54] A. Giddens, *The Nation-State and Violence* (Berkeley, CA: University of California Press, 1987).

[55] M. Glenny, *The Rebirth of History: Eastern Europe in the Age of Democracy* (London: Penguin Books, 1991).

[56] M. Glenny, *The Fall of Yugoslavia: The Third Balkan War*, 3rd rev. ed. (London: Penguin Books, 1996).

[57] P. Goedde, 'Global Cultures', in A. Iriye (ed.), *Global Interdependence: The World after 1945* (Cambridge, MA: The Belknap Press of Harvard University Press, 2014).

[58] K. Goldmann, U. Hannerz and Ch. Westin (eds), *Nationalism and Internationalism in the Post–Cold War Era* (London–New York: Routledge, 2000).

[59] P. S. Gorski, 'Pre-modern Nationalism: An Oxymoron? The Evidence from England', in G. Delanty and K. Kumar (eds), *The Sage Handbook of Nations and Nationalism* (London: Sage Publications, 2006).

[60] P. Gowan and P. Anderson (eds), *The Question of Europe* (London–New York: Verso, 1997).

[61] L. Greenfeld, *Nationalism: Five Roads to Modernity* (Cambridge, MA: Harvard University Press, 1992).

[62] L. Greenfeld, 'Is Nation Unavoidable? Is Nation Unavoidable Today?', in H. Kriesi et al. (eds), *Nation and National Identity: The European Experience in Perspective* (Zürich: Verlag Rüegger, 1999).

[63] L. Greenfeld, 'Modernity and Nationalism', in G. Delanty and K. Kumar (eds), *The Sage Handbook of Nations and Nationalism* (London: Sage Publications, 2006).

[64] L. van der Grift, *Securing the Communist State: The Reconstruction of Coercive Institutions in the Soviet Zone of Germany and Romania, 1944–1948* (New York: Lexington Books, 2011).

[65] Ernst B. Haas, *The Uniting of Europe: Political, Social and Economic Forces 1950–1957*, rev. ed. (Stanford, CA: Stanford University Press, 1958).

[66] John A. Hall (ed.), *The State of the Nation: Ernest Gellner and the Theory of Nationalism* (Cambridge: Cambridge University Press, 1998).

[67] M. Hechter, 'Internal Colonialism Revisited', in E. A. Tiryakian and R. Rogowski (eds), *New Nationalisms of the Developed West* (Boston, MA: Allen & Unwin, 1985).

[68] M. H. van Herpen, *Putin's Wars: The Rise of Russia's New Imperialism* (Lanham, MD: Rowman & Littlefield, 2014).

[69] E. J. Hobsbawm, *Nations and Nationalism since 1780. Programme, Myth, Reality* (Oxford: Oxford University Press, 1990).

[70] S. Hoffmann, 'Obstinate or Obsolete? The Fate of the Nation-State and the Case of Western Europe', in S. Hoffmann (ed.), *Conditions of World Order* (Boston, MA: Houghton Mifflin Company, 1968).

[71] S. Hoffmann, 'Reflections on the Nation-State in Western Europe Today', *Journal of Common Market Studies*, vol. 21, no. 1/2 (1982), pp. 21–37.

[72] C. Holbraad, *Internationalism and Nationalism in European Political Thought* (New York: Palgrave Macmillan, 2003).

[73] R. Holbrooke, *To End a War* (New York: Modern Library, 1998).

[74] L. Hooghe and G. Marks, 'A Postfunctionalist Theory of European Integration: From Permissive Consensus to Constraining Dissensus', *British Journal of Political Science*, vol. 39 (2008), pp. 1–23.

Bibliography

[75] S. M. Horak, 'Eastern European National Minorities, 1919–1980', in Stephan M. Horak et al., *East European National Minorities 1919–1980: A Handbook* (Littleton, CO: Libraries Unlimited, 1985).

[76] G.-H. Horn, *The Spirit of '68. Rebellion in Western Europe and North America, 1956–1976* (Oxford: Oxford University Press, 2007).

[77] M. Hroch, *Das Europa der Nationen. Die moderne Nationsbildung im europäischen Vergleich* (Göttingen: Vandenhoek & Ruprecht, 2005).

[78] S. P. Huntington, *The Clash of Civilizations and the Remaking of World Order* (New York: Simon & Schuster, 1996).

[79] A. Hurrel, *On Global Order: Power, Values, and the Constitution of International Society* (Oxford: Oxford University Press, 2007).

[80] M. Ignatieff, *Blood and Belonging: Journeys into the New Nationalism* (London: BBC Books, Chatto & Windus, 1993).

[81] A. Iriye, *Global and Transnational History: The Past, Present, and Future* (Basingstoke: Routledge, 2013).

[82] A. Iriye, 'The Making of a Transnational World', in A. Iriye (ed.), *Global Interdependence: The World after 1945* (Cambridge, MA: The Belknap Press of Harvard University Press, 2014).

[83] J. T. Ishiyama and M. Breuning, *Ethnopolitics in the New Europe* (Boulder, MA–London: Lynne Rienner Publishers, 1998).

[84] B. Jenkins and N. Copsey, 'Nation, Nationalism and National Identity in France', in B. Jenkins and S. A. Sofos (eds), *Nation & Identity in Contemporary Europe* (London–New York: Routledge, 1996).

[85] B. Jenkins and S. A. Sofos, 'Nation and Nationalism in Contemporary Europe: A Theoretical Perspective', in B. Jenkins and S. A. Sofos (eds), *Nation & Identity in Contemporary Europe* (London–New York: Routledge, 1996).

[86] Robert A. Jones, *The Soviet Concept of 'Limited Sovereignty' from Lenin to Gorbachev: The Brezhnev Doctrine* (Basingstoke-London: Macmillan, 1990).

[87] T. Judt, *Postwar: A History of Europe since 1945* (New York: The Penguin Press, 2005).

[88] H. Kaelble, 'Supranationalität in Europa seit dem Zweiten Weltkrieg', in H. A. Winkler and H. Kaelble (eds), *Nationalismus – Nationalitäten – Supranationalität* (Stuttgart: Klett-Cotta, 1993).

[89] W. Kaiser, *Christian Democracy and the Origins of the European Union* (Cambridge: Cambridge University Press, 2007).

[90] M. Kaldor, *New and Old Wars: Organized Violence in a Global Era*, 3rd ed. (Cambridge: Polity, 2012).

[91] E. Kamenka, 'Political Nationalism – The Evolution of the Idea', in E. Kamenka (ed.), *Nationalism: The Nature and Evolution of an Idea* (London: Edward Arnold).

[92] R. D. Kaplan, *Balkan Ghosts: A Journey through History* (New York: St Martin's Press, 1993).

[93] I. P. Karolewski and A. M. Suszycki, *The Nation and Nationalism in Europe: An Introduction* (Edinburgh: Edinburgh University Press, 2011).

[94]   M. T. Kaufman, 'Gorbachev Alludes to Czech Invasion', *New York Times*, 12 April 1987.

[95]   E. Kedourie, *Nationalism* (New York: Praeger, 1960).

[96]   R. King, *Minorities under Communism: Nationalities as a Source of Tension among Balkan Communist States* (Cambridge, MA: Harvard University Press, 1973).

[97]   H. Kohn, *The Idea of Nationalism: A Study in Its Origins and Background* (New York: The Macmillan Company, 1944).

[98]   P. Kopecký and C. Mudde, 'The Two Sides of Euroskepticism: Party Positions on European Integration in East Central Europe', *European Union Politics*, vol. 3, no. 3 (2002), pp. 297–326.

[99]   S. Kotkin, *Uncivil Society: 1989 and the Implosion of the Communist Establishment* (New York: Modern Library, 2010).

[100] S. D. Krasner, *Sovereignty: Organized Hypocrisy* (Princeton, NJ: Princeton University Press, 1997).

[101] Ch. Krauthammer, 'The Unipolar Moment', *Foreign Affairs*, vol. 70, no. 1 (1990–1), pp. 23–3.

[102] W. Kymlicka and K. Banting, *Multiculturalism and the Welfare State: Recognition and Redistribution in Contemporary Democracies* (Oxford: Oxford University Press, 2007).

[103] K. Larres (ed.), *A Companion to Europe since 1945* (Oxford: Wiley Blackwell, 2013).

[104] M. Laruelle, *Russian Nationalism and the National Reassertion of Russia* (London–New York: Routledge, 2009).

[105] M. Laruelle (ed.), *In the Name of the Nation–Nationalism and Politics in Contemporary Russia* (New York: Palgrave Macmillan, 2010).

[106] A. Lecours and G. Nootens, 'Understanding Majority Nationalism', in A.-G. Gagnon, A. Lecours and G. Nootens (eds), *Contemporary Majority Nationalism* (Montréal, QC–Kingston, ON: McGill-Queens's University Press, 2011).

[107] E. Lemberg, *Geschichte des Nationalismus in Europa* (Stuttgart: Curt E. Schwab, 1950).

[108] M. Lewin, *Russia/USSR/Russia: The Drive and Drift of a Super State* (New York: New Press, 1995).

[109] A. Lieven, 'The Weakness of Russian Nationalism', *Survival*, vol. 41, no. 2 (1999), pp. 53–70.

[110] J. Loughlin, 'British and French Nationalisms Facing the Challenges of European Integration and Globalization', in A.-G. Gagnon, A. Lecours and G. Nootens (eds), *Contemporary Majority Nationalism* (Montréal, QC–Kingston, ON: McGill-Queens's University Press, 2011).

[111] M. Malia, *The Soviet Tragedy–A History of Socialism in Russia, 1917–1991* (New York: Free Press, 1994).

[112] M. Mann, *The Dark Side of Democracy: Explaining Ethnic Cleansing* (New York: Cambridge University Press, 1995).

[113] M. Mann, 'A Political Theory of Nationalism', in S. Periwal (ed.), *Notions of Nationalism* (Budapest: Central European University, 1995).

Bibliography

[114] E. D. Mansfield and J. Snyder, *Electing to Fight: Why Emerging Democracies Go to War* (Cambridge, MA: MIT Press, 2005).

[115] S. Mau and C. Burkhardt, 'Migration and Welfare State Solidarity in Western Europe', *Journal of European Social Policy*, vol. 19, no. 3 (2009), pp. 213–29.

[116] J. Mayall, *Nationalism and International Society* (Cambridge: Cambridge University Press, 1993).

[117] M. Mazower, *Dark Continent: Europe's Twentieth Century* (New York: Knopf, 1999).

[118] M. Mevius, *Agents of Moscow: The Hungarian Communist Party and the Origins of Socialist Patriotism 1941–1953* (Oxford: Oxford University Press, 2005).

[119] M. Mevius, 'Reappraising Communism and Nationalism', *Nationalities Papers*, vol. 37, no. 4 (2009), pp. 377–400.

[120] D. Miller, *On Nationality* (Oxford: Clarendon Press, 1985).

[121] A. S. Milward, 'The Springs of Integration', in P. Gowan and P. Anderson (eds), *The Question of Europe* (London: Verso, 1997).

[122] A. S. Milward, *The European Rescue of the Nation State*, 2nd ed., with the assistance of George Brennan and Frederico Romero (London-New York: Routledge, 2000).

[123] A. Moravcsik, *The Choice for Europe. Social Purpose and State Power from Messina to Maastricht* (London: UCL Press, 1998).

[124] A. Moravcsik, 'What Can We Learn from the Collapse of the European Constitutional Project?', *Politische Vierteljahresschrift*, vol. 47, no. 2 (2006), pp. 219–41.

[125] E. Morozov, *The Net Delusion: How Not to Liberate the World* (London: Penguin Books, 2011).

[126] C. Mudde, *Populist Radical Right Parties in Europe* (Cambridge: Cambridge University Press, 2007).

[127] G. Myrdal, *Beyond the Welfare State: Economic Planning and Its International Implications* (New Haven, CT–London: Yale University Press, 1968).

[128] E. Nolte, *Die europäische Bürgerkrieg. Nationalismus und Bolschewismus* (Frankfurt am Main: Propyläen Verlag, 1987).

[129] P. Nora, 'Between Memory and History: Les Lieux de Mémoire', *Representations*, vol. 26, Special Issue: Memory and Counter-Memory (1989), pp. 7–24.

[130] N. O'Sullivan, *European Political Thought since 1945* (London: Palgrave Macmillan, 2004).

[131] P. Pananyi, 'Postwar Europe: A Continent Built on Migration', in K. Larres (ed.), *A Companion to Europe since 1945* (Oxford: Wiley Blackwell, 2013).

[132] B. Parekh, *Rethinking Multiculturalism: Cultural Diversity and Political Theory* (Basingstoke: Palgrave Macmillan, 2005).

[133] P. Pierson, *Dismantling the Welfare State? Reagan, Thatcher, and the Politics of Retrenchment* (New York: Cambridge University Press, 1995).

147

[134] R. Pipes, *Russia under the Old Regime* (Harmondsworth: Penguin, 1979).

[135] J. Plamenatz, 'Two Types of Nationalism', in E. Kamenka (ed.), *Nationalism: The Nature and Evolution of an Idea* (London: Edward Arnold, 1976).

[136] S. Plokhy, *The Last Empire: The Final Days of the Soviet Union* (London: One World, 2014).

[137] V. V. Putin, 'Annual Address to the Federal Assembly of the Russian Federation, April' (2005) (http://archive.kremlin.ru/eng/speeches/2005/04/25/2031_type70029type82912_87086.shtml) (accessed 6 April 2014).

[138] V. V. Putin, 'Meeting of the Valdai International Discussion Club, 19 September' (2013) (http://eng.kremlin.ru/news/6007) (accessed 6 December 2013).

[139] T. Rakowska-Harmstone, 'Nationalism and Integration in Eastern Europe: The Dynamics of Change', in T. Rakowska-Harmstone (ed.), *Communism in Eastern Europe* (Manchester: Manchester University Press, 1984).

[140] P. Ramet (ed.), 'The Interplay of Religious Policy and Nationalities Policy in the Soviet Union and Eastern Europe', in *Religion and Nationalism in Soviet East European Politics* (Durham, NC: Duke University Press, 1984).

[141] D. Remnick, *Resurrection: The Struggle for a New Russia* (New York: Random House, 1997).

[142] N. Riasanovsky, *Russian Identities: A Historical Survey* (Oxford: Oxford University Press, 2005).

[143] D. Rothermund, *The Routledge Companion to Decolonization* (London–New York: Routledge, 2006).

[144] T. Sarrazin, *Deutschland schafft sich ab. Wie wir unser Land aufs Spiel setzen* (Berlin: Deutsche Verlags-Anstalt, 2010).

[145] D. Sassoon, *One Hundred Years of Socialism: The West European Left in the Twentieth Century* (London–New York: I.B. Tauris, 1996).

[146] Th. Schieder, *Nationalismus und Nationalstaat. Studien zum nationalen Problem im modernen Europa*, eds. Otto Dann and Hans-Ulrich Wehler (Göttingen: Vandenhoeck & Ruprecht, 1991).

[147] H. Schulze, *Staat und Nation in der europäischen Geschichte* (München: C. H. Beck, 1994).

[148] W. Schumann and R. Müller, 'Integration als Problem internationaler Geschichte', in W. Loth and J. Osterhammel (eds), *Internationale Geschichte: Themen – Ergebnisse – Aussichten* (München: R. Oldenbourg Verlag, 2000).

[149] R. Scruton, 'In Defence of the Nation', in J. C. Clark (ed.), *Ideas and Politics in Modern Britain* (London: Macmillan, 1990).

[150] H. Seton-Watson, *Nations and States: An Inquiry into the Origins of Nations and the Politics of Nationalism* (London: Methuen, 1977).

[151] M. Shipway, *Decolonization and Its Impact: A Comparative Approach to the End of the Colonial Empires* (Oxford: Wiley-Blackwell, 2008).

[152] L. Silber and A. Little, *Yugoslavia: Death of a Nation*, rev. ed. (London: Penguin Books, 1997).

[153] G. Sluga, *Internationalism in the Age of Nationalism* (Philadelphia, PA: University of Pennsylvania Press, 2013).

[154] A. D. Smith, *Theories of Nationalism* (London: Holmes and Meier, 1971).

[155] A. D. Smith, *Nationalism in the Twentieth Century* (Oxford: Martin Robertson, 1979).

[156] A. D. Smith, *National Identity* (Harmondsworth: Penguin Books, 1991).

[157] A. D. Smith, *Nations and Nationalism in a Global Era* (Cambridge: Polity, 1996).

[158] A. D. Smith, 'Ethnicity and Nationalism', in G. Delanty and K. Kumar (eds), *The Sage Handbook of Nations and Nationalism* (London: Sage Publications, 2006).

[159] A. D. Smith, *Nationalism: Theory, Ideology, History*, 2nd ed. (Cambridge: Polity, 2010).

[160] T. Smith, *A Pact with the Devil: Washington's Bid for World Supremacy and the Betrayal of the American Promise* (New York: Routledge, 2007).

[161] J. Snyder, *From Voting to Violence: Democratization and Nationalist Conflict* (New York–London: W. W. Norton & Company, 2000).

[162] S. Strange, *The Retreat of the State: The Diffusion of Power in the World Economy* (Cambridge: Cambridge University Press, 1996).

[163] R. G. Suny, *The Revenge of the Past: Nationalism, Revolution, and the Collapse of the Soviet Union* (Stanford, CA: Stanford University Press, 1993).

[164] C. Sutherland, *Nationalism in the Twenty-First Century: Challenges and Responses* (Basingstoke: Palgrave Macmillan, 2012).

[165] A. Szczerbiak and P. A. Taggart, *Opposing Europe?* (Oxford: Oxford University Press, 2008).

[166] P. Taggart, *Populism* (Buckingham-Philadelphia, PA: Open University Press, 2000).

[167] Y. Tamir, *Liberal Nationalism* (Princeton, NJ: Princeton University Press, 1993).

[168] Ph. Ther and A. Siljak (eds), *Redrawing Nations: Ethnic Cleansing in East-Central Europe, 1944–1948* (Lanham, MD: Rowman and Littlefield, 2001).

[169] Ch. Tilly, *Big Structures, Large Processes, Huge Comparisons* (New York: Russel Sage Foundation, 1984).

[170] J. Tonge, *Northern Ireland* (Cambridge: Polity, 2006).

[171] Treaty Establishing the European Economic Community, Rome, March 1957 (http://en.wikisource.org/wiki/The_Treaty_establishing_the_European_Economic_Community).

[172] Treaty of Lisbon Amending the Treaty on European Union and the Treaty Establishing the European Community, signed at Lisbon, 13 December 2007 (http://eur-lex.europa.eu/).

[173] W. Wallace, 'Rescue or Retreat? The Nation State in Western Europe, 1945–93', *Political Studies*, xlii (1994), pp. 52–76.

[174] W. Wallace, 'The Nation-State – Rescue or Retreat?', in P. Gowan and P. Anderson (eds), *The Question of Europe* (London: Verso, 1997).

[175] B. Wasserstein, *Barbarism and Civilization: A History of Europe in Our Time* (Oxford: Oxford University Press, 2007).

[176] H.-U. Wehler, *Nationalismus. Geschichte – Formen – Folgen* (München: Verlag C. H. Beck, 2011).

[177] R. G. Wilkinson and K. Pickett, *The Spirit Level: Why More Equal Societies Almost Always Do Better* (London: Allen Lane, 2009).

[178] H. A. Winkler, 'Einleitende Bemerkungen', in H. A. Winkler and H. Kaelble (eds), *Nationalismus – Nationalitäten – Supranationalität* (Stuttgart: Klett-Cotta, 1993).

[179] H. A. Winkler, 'Nationalismus, Nationalstaat und nationale Frage in Deutschland seit 1945', in H. A. Winkler and H. Kaelble (eds), *Nationalismus – Nationalitäten – Supranationalität* (Stuttgart: Klett-Cotta, 1993).

[180] H. A. Winkler, *Geschichte des Westens. Die Zeit der Gegenwart* (München: C. H. Beck, 2015).

[181] H. A. Winkler and H. Kaelble (eds), *Nationalismus – Nationalitäten – Supranationalität* (Stuttgart: Klett-Cotta, 1993).

[182] A. Wirsching, *Der Preis der Freiheit. Geschichte Europas in unserer Zeit* (München: C. H. Beck, 2012).

[183] S. Woodward, *Balkan Tragedy: Chaos and Dissolution after the Cold War* (Washington, DC: Brookings Institution Press, 1995).

[184] C. Wurm, 'Die Integrations- und Europapolitik Frankreichs und Grossbritanniens seit 1945 im Vergleich', in H. A. Winkler and H. Kaelble (eds), *Nationalismus – Nationalitäten – Supranationalität* (Stuttgart: Klett-Cotta, 1993).

[185] B. Yack, *Nationalism and the Moral Psychology of Community* (Chicago, IL: The University of Chicago Press, 2012).

[186] P. Zwick, *National Communism* (Boulder, CO: Westview Press, 1983).

Index